Daniel R. (Daniel Reaves) Goodloe

A history of the Demonetization of Silver

Daniel R. (Daniel Reaves) Goodloe

**A history of the Demonetization of Silver**

ISBN/EAN: 9783743320475

Manufactured in Europe, USA, Canada, Australia, Japa

Cover: Foto ©ninafisch / pixelio.de

Manufactured and distributed by brebook publishing software
(www.brebook.com)

Daniel R. (Daniel Reaves) Goodloe

**A history of the Demonetization of Silver**

# A HISTORY

# DEMONETIZATION OF SILVER.

## BY DANIEL R. GOODLOE.

It is singular that with one recent exception every step taken in Europe and America looking to the demonetization of silver has been prompted by the fact that the market price was higher than the mint price of the silver bullion—in other words, by the difficulty of keeping the silver coin in circulation when the temptation was great to send it to the melting-pot or to clip and deface it.

Silver, prior to the Conquest, and for centuries afterwards, was the sole money standard of England. Gold was gradually introduced. The money of account was pounds, shillings, pence and farthings; but only shillings, pence and farthings were coined. The pound troy was originally the pound sterling, but it underwent various reductions until, by the forty-third of Queen Elizabeth, the pound troy was divided into 62 shillings, thus reducing the shilling to less than one-third of its original value. It has remained at this value ever since. Prior to the reign of Edward Third silver was the exclusive legal-tender. Its proportionate value to gold was far higher than at present. From the middle of the eleventh to near the middle of the sixteenth century the relative values of gold and silver were as 1 to 12½, and sometimes down or up to 1 to 10½. But these proportions differed slightly in different countries. There was a gradual rise in the value of gold in Europe from this time forward for some years, and so early as the year 1665 it touched the point of 1 to 15.10. Since the latter date, and up to the epoch of demonetization in the United States and Germany, the variation in the values of the two metals has never, except on two occasions, amounted to one ounce of silver. The exceptions are, that in the year 1751, silver rose to 14.15, but fell back the next year to 14.54, and thirty years later it rose to 14.42, but fell back immediately to 14.54. In 1789 gold was to silver as 1 to 14.75, and the next year it stood at 15.04. From that date to 1872 the variations never exceeded half an ounce.

Dr. Kelley, author of the "Universal Cambist," states that for many years prior to the year 1816, when the British Parliament demonetized silver, "the supply of silver currency was very irregular, and the coins, however correctly minted, soon became greatly deteriorated, insomuch that in the year 1774, they were declared to be no longer a legal-tender for more than £25, although they had been previously unlimited in this respect." This statement refers to the worn or clipped silver coins. Silver of full weight still remained a legal-tender.

In the House of Commons, March 22, 1816, "Mr. Grenfell wished to know whether any arrangement had been made on a subject of very great importance, he meant for the establishment of a better circulation of silver. * * * It was well known that there was nothing like a tower shilling in the country, but that the circulation was made up of Birmingham counterfeits, which swelled the criminal calendar, or by old 12 and 24 sous pieces imported from France when the temptation to import these pieces, which in France passed for only 10 and 20 sous, was so great (the profit being 20 per cent.), it would be perceived that the introduction of them was not less mischievous than the counterfeit coining. It was stated by the late Lord Liverpool that the price of silver was never so high but that the country might have a good coinage, but now the price of silver was not much above the mint price. He thought, therefore, that a new coinage might take place without danger, but at least some temporary measure should be adopted to remedy the evil."

April 10, 1816, Mr. Barring (afterwards Lord Ashburton), in reference to the state of facts which Mr. Grenfell repeated, said:

"A measure which he should suggest would be to alter the standard of the silver currency so that it might not be carried out of the country on every slight variation of the price of that metal." He proposed a reduction of 10 *per cent.* in the amount of silver in the coin. He stated that the mint was in such a disgraceful condition that the officers, when they had a few tokens to make, knew nothing of the matter, and after many attempts all the dies were broken up.

May 28, 1816, the Prince Regent sent a message to the House of Commons announcing that he had given directions for an extensive issue of silver coins, and asked the assistance of the Commons in carrying the directions into effect.

May 30, Mr. Wellesly Pole explained the reason which moved the Regent to direct the new issue of silver coins. He said the time was favorable, universal peace existed, the balance of trade was in favor of the country, and the precious metals had fallen to their natural level. Silver was rather under the mint prices and gold very near it. There was no gold in circulation, and the silver coins were worn down to 30 per cent. below their nominal value. It had been found necessary to supply the deficiency of silver coin by an issue of bank tokens.

A high authority on the coins and currency of the realm was Lord Liverpool, who, in 1805, wrote a treatise on the subject, in the form of a letter to the King. He is quoted by the debaters in Parliament in 1816, and by subsequent writers, as a high authority. He informed His Majesty that, at the commencement of his reign (1760), crown pieces of silver had almost wholly disappeared, though at the general recoinage in King William's reign, 1695-'6, and afterwards, they had been coined to an amount of £1,553,047. Great numbers of the half crowns had also disappeared, and what remained were inadequate to the public needs. The amount coined had been £2,329,-

570. Those still in circulation were worn and impaired. The shillings coined in the same space of time amounted to £3,232,680. The six pences and smaller pieces coined amounted to £960,795. The smaller pieces had lost all trace of the impressions and marks of coinage. The causes of the impaired and deficient state of the silver coins were that the heavy pieces had been in general melted down or exported, and the remainder diminished by wear and filing. A considerable profit was derived from this latter practice, and very little silver bullion had been brought to the mint to be coined, "for the value of silver bullion as estimated at your Majesty's mint was lower compared with that of gold than the prices at which these metals respectively sold in the market."

These statements by English authorities can leave no doubt on any mind that silver at the current rate, was more valuable than gold in 1816, when silver was demonetized. That mint rate, according to Lord Liverpool, was a fraction over $15\frac{1}{4}$ to 1. His figures are $15\frac{2850}{3640}$. The market price was $14\frac{1}{4}$ to 1.

The act of 56 George Third, Chapter 68, A. D. 1816, reduced the subsidiary silver coin 6.45 per cent. below the legal standard. Silver bullion to be deposited by individuals was to be coined into crowns, half crowns, shillings, pence and farthings. The standard weight of the gold coins, and the old silver coins was $23\frac{1}{2}$ of pure metal and $\frac{1}{2}$ of alloy. In other words, 47 of pure metal to 1 of alloy. The new silver coinage under this act was eleven ounces two pennyweights of fine silver and eighteen pennyweights of alloy in the pound troy, and there were to be sixty-six instead of sixty-two shillings coined for every pound troy of metal.

In examining the authorities on this subject, including the debates in the two Houses of Parliament in 1816, I have been surprised to find no reference to the relative prices of gold and silver in the East—in India and China—as disturbing elements in the question. Yet the fact was well known to British statesmen that the precious metals in those countries in 1816 were held at almost the identical rates which prevailed in Europe in the middle ages. It is impossible to suppose that the immense trade which, even at that day, was carried on between England and her vast possession in Asia, could have been so conducted as not to effect the relative prices of gold and silver in England. "The wealth of nations" was published in 1776, forty years before the demonetization of silver in England. What the author says in regard to the relative values of the precious metals in his day in the East would be changed but little in so short a time, for the stability of Oriental manners, laws and customs is proverbial. The statements of Adam Smith, therefore, cannot fail to impress thoughtful minds with the idea that the high price of silver in India, and in China, had a great deal more effect upon the English markets, if not directly upon the English mind, in bringing about the demonetization of silver than English statesmen thought proper to avow.

Mr. Smith said :

"The precious metals are a commodity which it always has been and still continues to be extremely advantageous to carry from Europe to India. There is scarce a commodity which brings a better price there, or which in proportion to the quantity of labor and commodities it costs in Europe, will purchase or command a greater quantity of labor and commodities in India. It is more advantageous, too, to carry silver thither than gold, because in China and the greater part of the other markets of India, the proportion between fine silver and fine gold is but as ten, or at most as twelve to one; whereas, in Europe it is as fourteen or fifteen to one. In China and the greater part of the other markets of India, ten, or at most twelve ounces of silver, will purchase an ounce of gold; in Europe it requires from fourteen to fifteen ounces. In the cargoes, therefore, of the greater part of European ships which sail to India, silver has generally been one of the most valuable articles."

And, again, p. 346, vol. 2, he says :

"The great quantities of silver carried annually from Europe to India have, in some of the English settlements, gradually reduced the value of that metal in proportion to gold. In the mint of Calcutta an ounce of fine gold is supposed to be worth fifteen ounces of fine silver in the same manner as in Europe. It is in the mint perhaps rated too high for the value it bears in the market of Bengal. In China, the proportion of gold still continues as one to ten, or one to twelve. In Japan it is said to be as one to eight."

If the law in Calcutta was the same as that of England, it was of little consequence what the mint held gold and silver to be relatively worth, since the precious metals were only coined when deposited by individuals. Silver was the standard of value and legal-tender and very little gold was coined unless it were to be sent to England.

The clipped and filed coins in circulation in England, and the mass of crowns and half crowns which had been coined but could not be kept in circulation, which, as the writers and speakers of the day expressed it, were sent to the melting-pot, can all be accounted for by this statement of Adam Smith, by that of Lord Liverpool and by those of speakers in the House of Commons. The silver as bullion was shipped to India, China and Japan. The high value set on silver in those countries rendered it impossible to keep silver coins in circulation if made of standard silver. Mr. Barring, as the reader will have noticed, proposed a reduction of 10 per cent. in the amount of pure silver in the new coins. The English standard of purity of the precious metals since Elizabeth's time has been 23½ of pure metals to ½ of alloy. The great demand for small coin would keep the silver coins thus reduced in weight in the country. For it is the heavy coins that take wings and fly away, thus reversing a law of nature.

The act of 1816 provides—"That gold coins shall be in future the sole standard and measure of value and legal-tender of payment without any limitation of amount, and that silver coins shall be a legal-tender for the limited amount of forty shillings only at any one time."

No further movement looking to the demonetization of silver or of gold took place in any part of the world until after the discovery and development of the gold mines of California and Australia. The effect of the large increase in the amount of gold from those sources was to reduce its value with reference to other things, including silver; and this effect prompted speculative writers to discuss the question of demonetizing gold. The German states, including Austria, in 1857, acted on this idea, and demonetized the superabundant, though more precious metal, and declared silver to be the standard coin and legal-tender. But the reign of silver was brief; the discovery and development of the Nevada silver mines, a few years later, turned the scale. The same class of writers and statesmen who had demanded the demonetization of gold now turned their batteries against silver; and in December, 1871, the newly-organized German Empire, among its earliest important measures, decided to dethrone silver and make gold the standard of values and legal-tender.

On the 23d of December, 1865, France, Italy, Switzerland and Belgium, being contiguous countries, and all of them already on the double standard, and at the same ratio of 15½ to 1, between silver and gold, formed the monetary treaty known as the Latin Union. The object of the treaty was to make the coins of each a practically current money in all of them, which was accomplished by the agreement of each country to accept for taxes the coins of the other countries. As the smaller coins of all of them was below standard, it was stipulated that the amount of such coinage should be limited to a certain number of francs, and that when the treaty expired each government should give back full tender and full standard coins for its subsidiary coins held by the other governments.

In the year 1867 an international conference was held in Paris on the monetary question, the leaders in which were inspired by the desire to demonetize silver. Samuel B. Ruggles, of New York, representing the Chamber of Commerce of that city, was present to represent the United States. Mr. Sherman, of Ohio, chairman of the Finance Committee of the United States Senate, was in Paris at the time. Mr. Ruggles, in a letter dated May 17, informed the Senator that the current of opinion in the conference was "running strongly in favor of adopting as the unit the existing French five-franc piece of gold." Mr. Sherman replied, in a letter of the 18th, that—"If this is done France will surely abandon the impossible effort of making two standards of value. Gold coins will answer all the purposes of Europe. * * * They [the United States] could not agree upon the silver standard."

The Paris conference recommended the adoption by the nations of the gold standard.

Mr. Sherman, January 6, 1868, introduced a bill in relation to the coinage of gold and silver. It was referred to the Finance Committee. June 9 he made a report in favor of the bill. (S. No. 217.)

In this document he declares the object to be the adoption of a common monetary standard among commercial nations; that gold was practically demonetized in this country by the suspension of specie payments, and that the time was favorable for making a change in the coinage system.

The report proceeds to state. "The single standard of gold is an American idea, yielded reluctantly by France and other countries where silver is the chief standard of value. The impossible attempt to maintain two standards of value has given rise to nearly all the debasement of coinage of the last two centuries. The relative market value of silver and gold varied like other commodities, and this led first to the demonetization of the more valuable metal, and second, to the debasement or diminution of the quantity of that metal in a given coin. In a short time the cheaper metal would, by a diminished supply, become the dearer metal, and then it would be debased and cheapened in the same way. The process repeatedly occurred in Europe, and has twice occurred in the United States within the life of the present generation. By the act of June 28, 1834, our gold coin was reduced from 27 grains of standard gold to 25.8 grains, or 4.4 per centum, in order to make it correspond with the market value of silver. In consequence of the discovery of gold in California that metal was cheapened, and silver became relatively more valuable, and was hoarded or exported. To avoid this, the weight of our silver coin was reduced by the act of January 21, 1853, from 206 grains [in the half dollar] of standard silver to 192 grains, or 6.7 per centum."

It is proper to state that the reduction in the value of silver here referred to affected only what is known as the subsidiary coin—the halves, quarters, dimes and half dimes. The reason assigned for this reduction was that silver, in the proportions established by law, was more valuable than gold, and that the reduction in weight had become necessary in order to prevent the exportation of the minor coins, which were so essential to the daily uses of the people in all minor business transactions. The silver dollar, the unit of value, was less necessary to make change, as bank bills and gold answered the purpose. It was only coined at that time at the request of depositors of the silver bullion, and the inducement to the coinage of silver was very slight when gold was the cheaper metal.

It is singular that Mr. Sherman, after deprecating the debasement of the coin in his report, should propose in the bill which accompanied the report a further debasement of the coins to almost as great a degree as that of 1834. The first section of the bill (S. No. 217) provides:

"That with a view to promote a uniform currency among the nations the weight of the gold coin of five dollars shall be one hundred and twenty-four and nine-twentieths troy grains, so that it shall agree with a French coin of twenty-five francs, and with the weight of thirty-one hundred francs to the kilogram, and the other sizes and denominations shall be in due proportions of weight, and the fineness shall be nine-tenths, or nine hundred parts fine in one thousand.

"SEC. 2. That in order to conform the silver coinage to this rate, and to the French valuation, the weight of the half-dollar shall be one hundred and seventy-nine grains, equivalent to one hundred and sixteen decigrams ; and the lesser coins shall be in due proportion, and the fineness shall be nine-tenths. *But the coinage of silver pieces, of one dollar, five cents and three cents shall be discontinued.*"

"SEC. 6. *Provided,* That the foreign gold coins which conformed to these conditions should be a legal-tender in all payments whatsoever, so long as the standard of weight and fineness should be duly maintained."

Mr. Sherman, in his report, arraigned the double standard for causing a reduction in the weight of the gold dollar from 27 grains of standard gold to 25.8. And, then, in order to arrive at the single gold standard and to please the *doctrinaires* who attended the Paris conference, he proposed in his bill to reduce the weight of the gold dollar from 25.8 grains to 24.89. This result, the intelligent reader will arrive at by dividing the weight assigned by him for the half eagle, or five dollar piece by five.

In like manner he proposed a reduction of the weight of the subsidiary silver coin from 192 grains in the half dollar to 179.

Mr Morgan, then a Senator from New York, and a member of the committee, opposed the bill on account of these reductions in the weight of the coins, as well as on account of the demonetization of the silver dollar. In his minority report said :

"The reduction which this measure would effect in the present legal standard of the gold coin of the United States would be at the rate of three and a half dollars in the hundred ; and the reduction in the legal value of our silver coinage would be still more considerable." He urged other objections to the bill.

The bill provided for the coinage of silver halves, quarters, and dimes only ; and the third section provided that "the silver coins shall be a legal-tender to an amount not exceeding ten dollars in any one payment ;" while " the gold coins to be issued under this act shall be a legal-tender in all payments to any amount."

The act of January 18, 1837, provides that standard gold and silver shall consist of 900 parts pure metal and 100 parts alloy ; that the alloy of the gold coin is silver and copper, and the alloy of the silver coin is to be copper. These conditions are adopted in Mr. Sherman's bill.

The bill was ordered to be printed, and referred to the Committee on Finance. June 9th it was reported back with amendments. The first section made the five dollar gold piece of $124\frac{9}{10}$ grains troy equivalent to a coin of twenty five francs, and with the rate of six hundred and twenty dollars to the kilogram.

This bill, as amended, was very cunningly devised for the purpose of demonetizing silver without awakening the body-politic to a consciousness of the operation. It provided for gold coinage, *ad libertum*, at the pleasure of depositors of bullion at the mint. Gold was made a legal-tender to the fullest extent where coin was not specified ; silver bullion was to be purchased by Government for coinage into subsidiary coins and to be a legal tender in sums not exceeding five dollars. Silver bullion could not be deposited by individuals for coinage. No direct reference was made in the bill to the silver dollar ; but section 18 provided that no coins, either of gold or silver or minor coinage, shall hereafter be issued from the mint other than those of the denominations, standards and weights " herein set forth."

The amendment of the third section, instead of making the gold coins to be issued under the act a legal-tender in all payments to any amount, adds, "except for such existing bonds of the United States as are payable in coin."

This bill failed to become a law. There was no debate, and the important feature, the demonetization of silver, failed to attract notice, although it had been discussed in Mr. Sherman's report. The public men of that day appear to have been as unconcerned about the precious metals as men in general are in regard to the speculation of philosophers about a plurality of peopled worlds. Neither gold nor silver had been seen for a dozen years ; and no one expected to live to see either metal circulating as a currency. It was therefore deemed an idle consumption of time to consider the relative values of the two metals.

The next move in behalf of the demonetization of silver came from the Treasury Department in the form of a report and bill from Mr. Knox, the Comptroller of the Currency, indorsed by Mr. Boutwell, the Secretary. Mr. Sherman, chairman of the Committee on Finance in the Senate, introduced it in that body December 19, 1870. Dr. Linderman, the Director of the Mint, interposed in its behalf, and modestly assuming the prerogative of the President, recommended its passage. There was no discussion upon the main feature of the bill—the demonetization of silver. The long debate turned upon the minor question of a tax on coinage. The yeas, upon the passage of the bill, January 10, 1871, were as follows:

Yeas—Messrs. Bayard, Boreman, Brownlow, Casserly, Cole, Conkling, Corbett, Davis, Gilbert, Hamlin, Harlan, Jewett, Johnson, Kellogg, McCreery, Morton, Nye, Patterson, Pomeroy, Pool, Ramsay, Rice, Saulsbury, Spencer, Stewart, Stockton, Sumner, Thurman, Tipton, Trumbull, Vickers, Warner, Willey, Williams, Wilson, and Yates.—36.

Nays—Messrs. Abbott, Ames, Anthony, Buckingham, Carpenter, Chandler, Fenton, Hamilton, of Texas, Harris, Howell, Morrill, of Vermont, Pratt, Scott and Sherman.—14.

Absent—Messrs. Cameron, Cattell, Cragin, Edmunds, Ferry, Flanagan, Fowler, Hamilton, of Maryland, Howard, Howe, Lewis, Mc-

Donald, Morrill, of **Maine**, Osborn, Revels, Robertson, **Ross**, **Sawyer**, Schurz, Sprague, Thayer and Windom.—22.

Mr. Boutwell, the Secretary of the Treasury, in his indorsement of the bill, as framed in his Department, reiterating the statement of Mr. Knox, **recommended** its passage on the ground that silver was worth in the **market** 3.12 per cent. more than gold, according to the legal **standard** weight of 15½ to 1.

The **debate on** this bill in the two Houses of Congress is curious, as illustrative of the utter obliviousness of members, of all shades of party (except its originators), of its real importance and latent purpose As has been **stated** above, the long debate in the Senate turned upon the question—the comparatively insignificant question—whether the depositors of **bullion** should be taxed, or made to pay for coinage. The tax, or **charge,** was expected to bring in $150,000, and on this point two days were consumed in senatorial debate without a solitary allusion to the **demonetization** of silver. In the House of Representatives the debate **took** a wider range, but no one, by accident or design, touched upon **the** essential features of the bill. Yet, as presented by Mr. Sherman, on the 28th of April, 1870, it contained the following clauses, which no Senator proposed to change, and which were passed by a vote of 36 yeas to 14 nays. Strange to say, Mr. Sherman himself, **the** godfather of the bill voted against it, after urging its passage, because his amendment for taxing the coinage three-tenths of 1 per cent. failed to be adopted **as** a part of the bill. The amended bill was numbered, Senate No. 859. It provided—

"**Sec.** 14. That **the** twenty-dollar gold piece, or double eagle, should weigh 516 grains—nine-tenths of pure metal and one-tenth alloy. The eagle, or ten-dollar piece, was to weigh 258 grains; the half eagle, or five-dollar piece, was to weigh 129 grains; the quarter eagle, or two dollar and **a** half piece, was to weigh 64½ grains. The three-dollar piece was **to weigh** 77.4 grains; and the one-dollar piece, 25.8 grains." The **same** section also provided that **these** coins should be "**a** legal-**tender** in all payments."

**Section 15 provided** that of the silver coins, the weight of **the** half-dollar, or piece of **fifty** cents, shall be 192 grains; the quarters and **dimes were to** be respectively the half and the fifth part of the fifty **cent piece.** And the silver coin to be issued in conformity with this law was to be a legal-tender for all sums **less** than *one dollar.*

It will be noticed that these amendments to Mr. Sherman's, or the Treasury Department bill, fixed **the weights** of the coins as they existed prior to that date, and not as Mr. Sherman had fixed them **in** his bill of 1868. In other words, he found it necessary to **give** up the scheme **of reducing** them **to** the **level** of the French coins.

Sections 16 and **17 provided** for the coinage of the nickel and copper coins.

"**Sec.** 18. *That no coins, either of gold or silver or minor coinage, shall hereafter be issued from the mint other than those of the denominations, standards, and weights herein set forth.*"

The bill was sent to the House of Representatives and, on motion of Mr. Kelley, was read twice January 11, 1871, and ordered to be printed, and referred to the Committee on Coinage, &c.

February 24, Mr. Kelley reported back the bill from the Committee on Coinage, with an amendment in the nature of a substitute. The substitute is identical with the original bill as it regards the demonetization of silver. The eighteenth section remains unchanged. To the section making gold coins a "legal-tender in all payments," is added the words, "at their denominational value." The substitute extends the legal-tender power of silver from *one to five dollars*.

Nothing further was done with the bill during that session—the third session—which terminated on the 4th of March—the end of the Forty-first Congress.

January 8, 1872, Mr. Kelley, by unanimous consent, submitted the following resolution, which was read, considered and adopted:

"*Resolved*, That the Committee on Coinage, Weights and Measures be instructed to inquire and report whether the intrinsic value of the silver coinage, as compared with the gold coinage, is not above that of other nations, and greater than is necessary for coins designed for subsidiary purposes only, and to be retained permanently in the country; also whether it would not be proper to exact seigniorage from the silver coinage equal to the cost of fabrication, distribution, and recoinage at the public expense of coins worn by natural abrasion below the legal standard weight; and whether the requiring of such a seigniorage would not reduce the standard of the silver coined to an extent sufficient to prevent their exportation as bullion in the ordinary fluctuation of the bullion market, and give the public the advantage for purposes of change to be limited as to the amount of legal-tender and issue."

January 9, 1872, Mr. Kelley, from the Committee on Coinage, Weights and Measures, reported back with the recommendation that it do pass the bill (H. of R. No. 5). This bill was identical with that which passed the Senate at the preceding session as it regards the regulating and restricting the coinage of silver, as Mr. Kelley's explanation of its contents will show. Like its predecessors of 1868 and 1870-'71, in the Senate, it contained the section which limited the coinage of silver to what is known as subsidiary coin, the legal-tender quality of which was limited to five dollars. It also contained the eighteenth section, which forbade the coinage of silver dollars.

On the same day Mr. Kelley said: "I desire that the bill shall be fairly considered. It is not a pet measure of my own. It is a measure originated by the Treasury Department, and growing out of the necessities of the case. The mint law of this country has never been revised. * * * Time as well as circumstances has tended to make the law somewhat, I may say, with propriety, incoherent or crude. The Secretary of the Treasury, discovering the difficulty of administering the affairs of so many mints and assay-offices, gave the subject his personal consideration, and then invited to his aid some of the most experienced gentlemen in the country in the matters of coinage and the management of the mints, and directed one of the officers of the Treasury, in connection with those gentlemen, to codify the mint laws. That was done, and the codification with such suggestions as those commissioners, as I may call them, made, were submitted to the two Houses of Congress. The Senate took up the bill and acted upon it during the last Congress, and sent it to this House. It was referred to the Committee on Coinage, Weights and Measures, and received as careful attention as I have ever known a committee to bestow upon any measure. The committee, before proceeding to consider it, sent copies of it, not to the Director of the Mint alone, but to the officers of all the mints, and to those gentlemen who, within the last fifteen or twenty years, have been connected with the mints, and made reputations which justified the committee in attaching importance to their opinions and the results of their experience; and thus enlightened from sources to which the Secretary had not applied, the committee proceeded with great deliberation to go over the bill, not only section by section, but line by line, and word by word."

This statement of Mr. Kelley, the reader will take notice, refers to what was done by the two Houses during the preceding Congress. He proceeds to say :

"The bill has not received the same elaborate consideration from the Committee on Coinage, Weights and Measures of this House, but the attention of each member was brought to it at the earliest day of this session ; each member procured a copy of the bill, and there has been a thorough examination of the bill again. I think that when the House comes to consider the bill, while they may find some amendments to make that would be judicious, *they will find the body of the bill to be a well-devised and careful codification of the mint laws, making a very few, if any essential changes, except in this—* there is now a Director of the Mint ; his office is attached to the mint at Philadelphia, and there is no more reason why he should supervise the other mints than there is that the chief officers of the other mints should supervise him. There is really no subordination, there is no responsible head to our mints, or our system of coinage ; and if the law be not brought into better shape than it is, we shall perhaps, without willful fault on the part of any body, find our coinage one that other nations may not recognize or that we ourselves doubt." Mr. Kelley failed to add what he seems to have intended to say, that the bill made the mint a bureau of the Treasury Department, with the officers of the mint directly subordinate to the Secretary. This he represented as the only essential change made by the bill in the laws relating to the mints and coinage.

Mr. Kelley called attention to the fact that the bill was proposed in 1871, and that section 72 read : "This act shall be known as the coinage act of 1871." He moved to strike out "1871" and insert "1872."

Mr. POTTER, of New York, said : " I desire in the first place to ask the gentleman who has this bill in charge whether, if it become a law, it will make any change in the value of the coin issued pursuant to its provisions from the value of the coin which now exists?"

" Mr. KELLEY. It does not."

" Mr. Kelley. * * * *This bill is a mere* codification. There are one or two things in this bill, I will say to the gentleman from New York, with his permission, which I personally would like to modify ; *that is to say, I would like to follow the example of England, and make a* **wide** *difference between our silver and gold coinage. But as I was charged with a bill that looked only to the codification of the mint laws,* or mainly to that, I did not feel it well to interject into that bill any of my own peculiar views. *I would have liked to make the gold dollar* **uniform** *with the French system* of weights, taking the grain as the unit."

It must be clear to every intelligent reader that Mr. Kelley could not have read carefully the bill which he introduced, and of which he urged the passage. It is true that it does not in terms declare the silver dollar to be no longer a legal-tender, but it was repeatedly asserted by the friends of the bill that the silver dollar had long ago gone out of existence—that in consequence of its superior value to the gold dollar it had been sent to the melting-pot ; and now, Mr. Kelley's bill, by the 18th section, prohibited its recoinage. But Mr. Kelley was not alone in his ignorance on this point. A large majority of both Houses was in the same benighted condition. There was at least one member present, Mr. Hooper, of Massachusetts, who could have corrected him, but it was not the policy of those who favored the demonetization of silver to call attention to the 18th section.

Messrs. Potter and Garfield complained of the continued issue of the subsidiary silver halves, quarters, &c., below the standard relative values of the two metals. Mr. Potter styled it "an untruthful coinage—a coinage that was not in value what it pretended to be ;" and Mr Garfield expressed the hope that " the time will come when we will not have tokens, but real money ; neither tokens in metal, nor tokens in paper, unless they represent their full value."

Yet, neither Mr. Garfield nor Mr. Potter said a word which could convey the inference that he was aware of the import of the eighteenth section of the bill. Mr. Potter, like Mr. Kelley, said that he favored the demonetization of silver, but neither of those highly intelligent gentlemen was aware that the bill accomplished that very result.

In the course of this debate Mr. POTTER charged that Mr. Kelley's interest in securing nickel coinage arose from the fact that the nickel was produced in Pennsylvania. Mr. Kelley repelled this charge.

But for some reason, which was not explained, Mr. Kelley's bill failed to satisfy the original movers in the work of the demonetization of silver.

Hence, February 9, 1872, Mr. Hooper, of Massachusetts, by unanimous consent, reported from the Committee of Coinage, Weights and

Measures another bill (H. R. No. 1427) revising and amending the laws of the United States relative to the mints, &c., which was read a first and second time, recommitted to the Committee of Coinage, &c., and ordered to be printed.

Mr. Holman moved to reconsider the vote by which the bill was recommitted, and also moved that the motion to reconsider be laid on the table. The latter motion was agreed to.

February 13, 1872, Mr. Hooper rose to make a report from the Committee on Coinage, Weights and Measures.

Mr. McNeeley, a member of the committee, knew of no bill having been acted on. He attended every meeting of the committee, and remembered nothing of the kind, and raised the question that this was not a report from the committee.

Mr. Hooper. The majority of the committee instructed me to make the report.

Mr. McNeeley had never seen a majority of the committee present. He hoped it would not be presented.

Mr. Kelley said he had authorized Mr. Hooper to act for him.

Mr. McNeeley denied that the bill was authorized to be reported by the committee.

The bill was made the special order for the second Tuesday in March, but was not reached on that day.

April 9, 1872, Mr. Stoughton called for the regular order, which the Speaker announced to be the bill (H. R. No. 1427) relative to the mints, assay offices, coinage, &c.

Mr. Hooper, of Massachusetts, addressed the House in explanation of its nature. He said:

"The bill was prepared two years ago, and has been submitted to careful and deliberate examination. It has the approval of nearly all the mint experts of the country, and the sanction of the Secretary of the Treasury. Mr. Ernest Sayd, of London, a distinguished writer, who has given great attention to the subject of mints and coinage, after examining the first draft of the bill, furnished many valuable suggestions which have been incorporated in the bill." Mr. Sayd had published a treatise in favor of bi-metallism; and any suggestion he may have made to Mr. Hooper on that point could not have been among those which were incorporated in the bill. Mr. Hooper proceeds to explain the bill, section by section, but only those affecting the relations of gold and silver to each other are here quoted. He says:

"Section thirteen defines the standard of fineness for gold and silver coin, making no change in the existing law, except to reduce the quantity of silver permitted to remain in the alloy of gold coins, which is not to exceed one-tenth of the whole alloy, instead of one-half, as now." * * *

"Section fourteen declares * * * the gold dollar of twenty-five and eight-tenths grains of standard gold to be the unit of value, gold practically having been in this country for many years the standard or measure of value, as it is legally in Great Britain and most of the European countries. The silver dollar, which by law is now the legally declared unit of value, *does not bear a correct relative proportion to the gold dollar. Being worth intrinsically about one dollar and three cents in gold, it cannot circulate concurrently with the gold coins.*

"*The silver dollar of four hundred and twelve and a half grains, by reason of its bullion or intrinsic value being greater than its nominal value, long since ceased to be a coin of circulation, and is melted by manufacturers of silverware.*"

"Section sixteen re-enacts the provisions of existing laws defining the silver coins and their weights respectively, *except in relation to the silver dollar, which is reduced in weight from four hundred and twelve and a half to three hundred and eighty-four grains, thus making it a subsidiary coin in harmony with the silver coins of less denomination to secure its concurrent circulation with them.*"

"*Section eighteen provides that no coins other than those prescribed in this act shall hereafter be issued.*"

Mr. POTTER, of New York, who, in January, when the bill of Mr. Kelley was before the House, gave intimation of his opposition, now saw reason to change his opinion, while he still thought that legislation with reference to coinage was out of place so long as specie payment was suspended. In regard to the demonetization of silver he said : "Then, in the next place, this bill provides for the making of changes in the legal-tender coin of the country, and for substituting a legal-tender coin of only one metal instead, as heretofore, of two. I think, myself, this would be a wise provision, and that legal-tender coins, except subsidiary coin, should be of gold alone; but why should we legislate on this now when we are not using either of those metals as a circulating medium? The bill provides also for a change in respect of the weight and value of the silver dollar, which I think is a subject which, when we come to require legislation about it at all, will demand at our hands very serious consideration, and which, as we are not using such coins for circulation now, seems at this time to be an unnecessary subject about which to legislate."

Mr. KELLEY charged that a certain man in New York city was making many thousands a year by depositing silver bullion for coinage into halves, quarters, &c., which contained less than the standard proportion of silver to gold. His remedy was to reduce the silver dollar to the same condition by depriving it of its legal-tender value. Yet, on the same occasion, Mr. Kelley said : "The silver dollar required by our laws is worth three and a half cents more than our gold dollar, and is worth seven cents more than two half dollars."

April 9, 1872, Mr. STOUGHTON, of Michigan, called for the regular order, which was the bill (H. R. No. 1427) revising the laws relative to the mint, coinage, etc.

Mr. STOUGHTON. Mr. Speaker, the bill under consideration is intended to be a complete revision of the laws pertaining to the mint and coinage of the United States. The existing laws upon this subject are embraced in different enactments extending over the whole period of time since the act of April 2, 1792. Some of these are obsolete and others repealed or changed by later laws. It has been the aim of the committee to arrange, compile, and codify the laws now in force in a systematic form, and to supply such deficiencies as the enlarged wants of the public seemed to indicate. Mr. Stoughton stated that the bill made gold coins the legal-tender for all sums and restricted the legal-tender character of silver to sums not above five dollars. He assigned as a reason for this that "the value of silver depends in a great measure upon the fluctuations of the market and the supply and demand." It seems not to have occurred to him that gold was subject to the same fluctuations in value which depend upon the supply and demand ; and that in the particular case in hand it was the gold that had fallen in value while silver remained stationary relatively to other commodities. He repeated the statements of Messrs. Hooper and Kelley, that " *the silver dollar, as now issued, is worth for bullion three and one-fourth cents more than the gold dollar*, and seven and one-fourth cents more than two half [silver] dollars."

Mr. **Kelley**, on the same day, after stating as a reason for demonetizing silver, that it was worth above three cents in the dollar more than gold, according to the standard rate, said : "You cannot determine this year what will be the relative values of gold and silver next year. They were fifteen to one a short time ago, they are sixteen to one now." It is evident that Mr. Kelley's ideas on the subject were a little confused when he assumed that a rise in the bullion value of silver above the standard mint value was to have the effect of increasing the distance between the two metals.

The reader will feel surprised that these frank statements of Messrs. Hooper, Kelley, Stoughton and Potter failed to arouse the vast majority of the House to a consciousness of what was going on. Yet such was the fact. Not more than half a dozen members seem to have understood the import of the terms used when they were told that gold, in the distant future, was to be the exclusive standard of value and legal-tender. This melancholy fact will fully appear in the sequel. And, strange to say, Mr. Kelley, himself, will be found among those who confessed their ignorance of what was going on.

May 27, Mr. HOOPER called up the bill (H. R. 1427) revising and amending the laws relative to mints, coinage, etc., and moved a substitute (H. R. 2934). He stated that he had submitted it to different gentlemen in the House who had taken an interest in the bill. " I find that it meets with universal approbation in the form in which I offer it. I move that the rules be suspended and that the substitute be put on its passage."

Mr. **Brooks**. I ask the gentleman from Massachusetts [Mr. Hooper] to postpone his motion until his colleague on the committee, my colleague from New York [Mr. Potter], is in his seat. It is my opinion that he does not concur in this substitute.

Mr. Hooper [of Massachusetts]. It is so late in the session that I must decline waiting any longer.

Mr. Holman. I suppose it is intended to have the bill read before it is put upon its passage.

The Speaker. The substitute will be read.

Mr. Hooper, of Massachusetts. *I hope not. It is a long bill, and those who are interested in it are perfectly familiar with its provisions.*

Mr. Kerr, of Indiana. The rules cannot be suspended so as to dispense with the reading of the bill?

The Speaker. They can be.

Mr. Kerr. *I want the House to understand* that it is *attempted to put through this bill without being read.*

The Speaker [Mr. Blaine]. Does the gentleman from Massachusetts [Mr. Hooper] move that the reading of the bill be dispensed with?

Mr. Hooper. I will so frame my motion to suspend the rules that it will dispense with the reading of the bill.

The Speaker. The gentleman from Massachusetts moves that the rules be suspended, and that the bill pass, the reading thereof being dispensed with.

Mr. Randall. Cannot we have a division of that motion?

The Speaker. A motion to suspend the rules cannot be divided.

Mr. Randall. I should like to have the bill read, although I am willing that the rules should be suspended as to the passage of the bill.

The question was put on suspending the rules and passing the bill without reading; and, two-thirds not voting in favor thereof, the rules were not suspended.

After some intervening business of a different nature—

Mr. Hooper. I now move that the rules be suspended, and the substitute for the bill in relation to mints and coinage be passed, and I ask that the substitute be read.

The clerk began to read the substitute.

Mr. Brooks. Is that the original bill?

The Speaker. The motion of the gentleman from Massachusetts applies to the substitute, and that on which the House is called to act is being read.

Mr. Brooks. As there is to be no debate the only chance we have to know what we are doing is to have both the bill and the substitute read.

The Speaker. The motion of the gentleman from Massachusetts being to suspend the rules and pass the substitute, it gives no choice between the two bills. The House must either pass the substitute or none.

Mr. Brooks. How can we choose between the original bill and substitute unless we hear them both read?

The Speaker. The gentleman can vote "ay" or "no" on the question whether this substitute shall be passed.

The opposition to this summary method of passing the bill, surrendered the point, after a few questions in regard to details, none of them, however, touching the main question, in regard to demonetization.

"The question being taken on the motion of Mr. Hooper, of Massachusetts, to suspend the rules and pass the bill, it was agreed to; there being ayes 110, noes 13."

The yeas and nays were not recorded.

May 28, 1872, the bill was sent to the Senate, but was not acted on during the session.

### IN THE SENATE, THIRD SESSION, *December* 16, 1872.

Mr. SHERMAN. I am directed by the Committee on Finance, to whom was referred the bill (H. R. No. 2934) revising and amending the laws relative to the mints and assay-offices and coinage of the United States, to report it back with two or three amendments. The amendments were ordered to be printed.

January 7, 1873, Mr. SHERMAN reported further amendments, and moved that the original bill be printed with the amendments. The motion was agreed to.

January 17, 1873, Mr. SHERMAN moved that the Senate proceed to the consideration of the Mint bill, which motion was agreed to.

The secretary proceeded to read the bill, but before concluding the Vice-President directed him to suspend, as the morning hour had expired. After some intervening business, Mr. Sherman called up the Mint bill. He thought it would occupy little more time than would be consumed in the reading. But some hours were spent in its consideration. No question was raised, however, upon the limitation of the legal-tender of silver, nor upon the stoppage of the coinage of silver dollars. On the same day the bill was read a third time and passed, with amendments. The House, January 23, nonconcurred in the Senate amendments, and asked for a committee of conference. The Speaker, January 25, announced as members of the committee: Mr. Hooper, of Massachusetts, Mr. McNeele, of Illinois, and Mr. Stoughton, of Michigan, on the part of House. The Senate adhered to its amendments, and named Messrs. Sherman, of Ohio, Scott, of Pennsylvania, and Bayard, of Delaware, as members of the committee.

February 6, the conference committee made their report in the Senate. Among the changes made by the substitute for the H. R. No. 1427 was to substitute a "trade-dollar" for the dollar of 392 grains. The trade-dollar, while containing 420 grains troy, was not to be a legal-tender except as subsidiary coin for $5.

The eighteenth section of the original bill became the seventeenth in the substitute, and forbade the coinage of standard legal-tender silver dollars.

The owners of gold bullion might deposit it, to any extent, to be coined into legal-tender currency. The owners of silver bullion could deposit the same for coinage into trade-dollars or into bars. The trade-dollars and bars were for exportation.

The report was agreed to by each House, and was approved the same day, February 12, 1873, by President Grant.

It had been stated, on the authority of Messrs. Hooper and others, that the standard silver dollar, on account of its greater intrinsic value as bullion than the gold dollar, had gone out of circulation. That it had been melted up by silversmiths or exported, and that it had practically ceased to exist. But the friends of mono-metallism were not satisfied. They had declared the silver unit to be a nonenity, and yet they were afraid of its ghost. Accordingly, they smuggled a clause of direct demonetization into the Revised Statutes. Nothing can be easier than to smuggle into the body of the laws by this process of revisal, any selfish scheme. The Revised Code is, after years spent in compiling, adopted by a simple act of the two Houses, without more formality, and with as much expedition as attends the passage of a small private claim. No single member undertakes to go through the heavy volume. No member pretends to do so. The result has been that the following section was smuggled into the revisal of 1874 without the knowledge of a solitary member who would have had the courage to avow the guilty consciousness. The act adopting the code was passed June 20, 1874. The section which declared gold to be a legal-tender for all amounts was properly taken from the above act of February 12, 1873. But the following section deserves to be branded as a fraudulent interpolation, and as on a par with altering the terms of a deed or will.

"Sec. 3586. The silver coins of the United States shall be a legal-tender at their nominal value for any amount not exceeding five dollars in any one payment."

The act under which the revisal was made was entitled "an act to revise and consolidate the statutes of the United States, in force on the first day of December, Anno Domini one thousand eight hundred and seventy-three." The two Houses of Congress confided in the integrity and good faith of the revisers, and the result is seen in the incorporation of the above section, which had no existence in any act which had been passed prior to December 1st, 1873, nor subsequently thereto, until it was surreptitiously introduced into the Revisal.

The following statement, showing that the Revised Statutes were approved by Congress, under assurances of those who professed to know, that the work was strictly a revisal, and that it contained nothing additional to the existing laws, is worthy of special attention. On January 10, 1878, Mr. Beck, in the course of an elaborate speech on the silver question said: "The Revised Statutes came next, and every man who remembers the history of the revision will remember that every possible assurance was given by the managers of that bill that no change was or should be made by them in existing laws. Any provision of those statutes changing existing laws was and is a fraud upon the country, whether so intended or not, and should be now corrected as we would correct an error or change in an enrolled bill. At the first session of the Forty-third Congress the Revised Statutes were brought up, and when they were laid before the House the pledge was given in every conceivable form, by men who were managing the bill, that there should be no change made in the existing law, that no word should be used that could by any possibility alter the sense of any existing law, that to the dotting of the *i* and the crossing of the *t* the sense and the language should be retained as far as was consistent with making a proper collection of the statutes under proper headings." General Butler first laid them before the House, and said:

"I desire to premise here that your committee felt it their bounden duty not to allow, so far as they could ascertain, any change of the law. This embodies the law as it is. The temptation, of course, was very great where a law seemed to be imperfect to perfect it by the alteration of words and phrases, or to make some change, but that temptation has, so far as I know and believe, been resisted. We have not attempted to change the law in a single word or letter, so as to make a different reading or different sense. All that has been done has been to strike out the obsolete parts, and to condense and consolidate and bring together statutes *in pari materia*, so that you have here, except in so far as it is human to err, the laws of the United States under which we now live. And it will be necessary, if the bill passes Congress, that it shall pass without any one undertaking to amend the law as it stands in this revision, because once beginning to amend the revision by altering the law from what it is will lead into an interminable sea, in which we shall never find soundings, and which will never find a shore. But if there be any omission of any provision of law, the theory of this revision is that, that it shall be supplied, and to that the committee desire to call the attention of the House."

Mr. Poland, of Vermont, reiterated the same assurances in the most positive language.

It may very well happen that sins of omission may be the consequence of inadvertence, but the interpolation of a whole section into what purports to be, and what the law and officials oaths require to be an exact copy, could proceed from nothing short of deliberate design.

April 1, 1874, Senator Hawley, of Connecticut, recapitulated the ideas of his speech for resumption in these words, which clearly imply his ignorance of the fact that the coinage of the silver dollar had been prohibited. He said:

"1. The precious metals furnished the best standard of values for a medium of exchange.

"2. The proper currency is one composed of gold, silver, and paper, convertible on presentation into coin."

April 11, 1874, Mr. E. R. Hoar, of Massachusetts, then a member of the House of Representatives, seems to have been ignorant of the fact that the act of February 12, 1873, had prohibited the coinage of the silver dollar, as appears from the following amendment offered by him to a pending bill relating to the currency :

"That from and after the first day of September, 1874, nothing but gold and silver coin of the United shall be a legal-tender in the payment of any debt thereafter contracted."

This amendment may possibly have restored the silver dollar as a legal-tender ; but it would not have restored the right to coin ; while Mr. Sherman, chairman of the Finance Committee of the Senate, Dr. Linderman, of the Mint, and the Secretary of the Treasury concurred in declaring that there were no silver dollar extant.

December 21, 1874, Mr. SHERMAN, from the Committee of Finance, reported a bill (Senate, No. 1044) for the resumption of specie payments. It was taken up for consideration the following day.

Section first provided for the issue of subsidiary silver coin—halves, quarters and dimes to be a substitute for the fractional currency, and to be a legal-tender for sums not greater than five dollars.

Section second repeals the section of the coinage act which imposed a charge of one-fifth of one per cent. for coining gold.

Section third repeals the limitation upon the aggregate amount of the circulating notes of the national banks. To facilitate resumption, the legal-tender paper currency might be reduced in amount until the maximum should be $300,000,000 by the substitution of national bank bills. Eighty per cent. of the United States notes, or greenbacks, were to be redeemed or withdrawn from circulation for every hundred per cent. of bank bills issued. It was provided "that on and after the first day of January, 1879, the Secretary of the Treasury shall redeem in coin, at the office of the assistant treasurer, in New York, the legal-tender notes then outstanding in sums of not less than fifty dollars." And to enable the Secretary of the Treasury to prepare and provide for the redemptions authorized by the act he was authorized to use the surplus revenue in the Treasury not otherwise appropriated, and to sell and dispose of, at not less than par in coin, either of the descriptions of bonds described in the act of July 4, 1870, entitled an act for refunding the national debt.

The intelligent reader is aware that the act of 1862, for borrowing $500,000,000, was on the basis of paying the interest in coin—gold and silver coin—while nothing was said about redeeming the principal in coin. It was maintained by many, including Thaddeus Stevens and John Sherman, then members of the House of Representatives, that the principal of the public debt, the five-twenties might lawfully be paid in United States legal-tender notes. On the other hand, it was contended by the bond-holders and by many others, that such was not the understanding when the loans were put upon the market. The Secretary of the Treasury, in the act of issuing the bonds, declared by public advertisement that they were to be redeemed in coin, and this seems to have been a fair inference from the very act of Congress of 1862 which authorized the first loan. That act created, or authorized, a sinking fund, for the avowed purpose of redeeming the bonds in coin. Congress at length adopted this view of the case, and in 1869 a declaratory act was passed, which pledged the faith of the nation to redeem the bonds in coin; but coin then meant gold and silver, and on this basis resumption would have been far easier than it became when gold was made the sole legal-tender. But the bond-holders and creditor classes who for years had trembled in their shoes under the threats of Messrs. Stevens, Sherman and others, that the bonds and all debts were to be paid in greenbacks, were now emboldened to demand gold exclusively. This demand came first from the other side of the Atlantic, where the largest part of the public debt was held, and where gold was the exclusive standard of value. English capitalists found means of influencing public men in America, and of bringing over to their views and interests even some "Greenbackers," no less than capitalists. The result of this foreign influence upon American affairs is seen in the acts above described, the demonetization of silver by fraud and the resumption of specie payments in gold in violation of the original contracts, public and private.

This resumption act was passed in the Senate the day following its introduction—December 22, 1874,—by yeas 32, nays 14, absent 27. This was on the eve of Christmas, and the bill was not taken up in the House until January 7; it was passed in that body without amendment, yeas 136, nays 98, absent 54. The vote was not a test in either House, as some voted against the bill or abstained from voting, for one reason or another, who were in favor of resumption. The bill was signed January 14, 1875.

March 30, 1876, the question being on Mr. Sherman's bill to take away the legal-tender character of the trade-dollar and reduce it to the category of minor coins:

"Mr. CONKLING. Will the Senator allow me to ask him, or some other Senator, a question? Is it true that there is now by law no American silver dollar; and if so, is it true that the effect of this bill is to be to make half-dollars and quarter dollars the only silver coin which can be used as a legal-tender?"

"Mr. SHERMAN. I will answer the Senator from New York, that since the law of 1853, the use of the silver whole dollar has been discontinued and none has been issued. That has been so since 1853."

"Mr. CONKLING. Is there power to issue it?"

"Mr. SHERMAN. There is no power and has been none."

Messrs. Bogy and Jones, of Nevada, corrected this misstatement of Mr. Sherman; and it is strange that he should have been misinformed on the subject, and having that impression it is strange that in the several bills relating to the mints and coinage, which he introduced in 1868, 1870, 1871, and 1872, he was careful to insert clauses prohibiting the coinage of silver dollars, if, as he believed, the prohibition was made by the act of 1853.

### PRESIDENT GRANT IGNORANT THAT SILVER HAD BEEN DEMONETIZED OR ITS COINAGE PROHIBITED.

The coinage of the silver dollar was prohibited February 12, 1873. On the 6th of October of that year President Grant wrote to Mr. Cowdry, a banker, as follows:

"I wonder that silver is not already coming into the market to supply the deficiency in the circulating medium. * * * Experience has proved that it takes about $40,000,000 of fractional currency to make the small change necessary for the transaction of the business of the country. Silver will gradually take the place of this currency, and further, will become the standard of values, which will be hoarded in a small way. I estimate that this will consume from $200,000,000 to $300,000,000, in time, of this species of our circulating medium. I confess to a desire to see a limited hoarding of money. It insures a firm foundation in time of need. But I want to see the hoarding of something that has a standard value the world over. Silver has this.

"Our mines are now producing almost unlimited amounts of silver, and it is becoming a question, 'what shall we do with it?' I suggest here a solution that will answer for some years—to put it in circulation, keeping it there until it is fixed and then we will find other markets."

January 14, 1875, six months after the adoption of the Revised Code, which demonetized the silver dollar, President Grant sent a message to Congress approving the Resumption Act, in which he said:

"With the present facilities for coinage, it would take a period probably beyond that fixed by law for final specie resumption to coin the silver necessary to transact the business of the country."

He therefore recommended the establishment of new mints at Chicago, Omaha, or St. Louis, and he thus showed his ignorance of the fact that he had signed an act which demonetized silver.

May 1, 1876, Mr. FROST, of Massachusetts, introduced a joint Resolution (H. R. 109) for the issue of silver coin, which was read a first and second time and referred to the committee on Banking and Currency and ordered to be printed.

May 2, Mr. PAYNE, of Ohio, by unanimous consent, submitted a report from the Committee of Banking and Currency, and upon the resolution which was referred to it yesterday in regard to silver coin. The clerk read the report as follows: "The Committee on Banking and Currency, to whom was referred the House Resolution No. 109, report the same back with the following amendment:"

"The SPEAKER pro tempore. The clerk will read resolution with the amendments in it as reported." The clerk read as follows:

"Resolved, &c., That the Secretary of the Treasury, under such limits and regulations as will best secure a just and fair distribution of the same throughout the country, may issue the silver coin now in the Treasury to an amount not exceeding $10,000,000 exchanged for an equal amount of legal-tender notes, and the notes so received in exchange shall be re-issued only upon the retirement and destruction of a like sum of fractional currency received at the Treasury in payment of dues to the United States, and said fractional currency when so substituted, shall be destroyed and held as part of the sinking fund, as provided in the act approved April 17, 1876."

The original resolution was unlimited as to the amount of silver coin that might be distributed. It was otherwise identical with the above.

Mr. Cox, of New York, from the same committee, called up the subject June 10 to report back a substitute, only differing from that reported by Mr. Payne by requiring the legal-tender notes taken in exchange for the $10,000,000 of silver, to be kept as a separate fund, until they could be canceled. In this form the joint resolution was passed.

On the same day Mr. Cox reported back from the Committee on Banking and Currency, with an amendment, the Randall bill. This bill (H. R. No. 2450) was introduced by Mr. Randall March 2, 1876. The first section makes an appropriation of $163,000 for engraving and printing. The second section authorizes the Secretary of the Treasury to issue silver coins of standard value of the denominations of ten cents, twenty, twenty-five and fifty cents, in redemption of an equal amount of fractional currency, whether the same were in the Treasury awaiting redemption, or wherever presented for redemption, and this process to be carried on until the whole amount of outstanding fractional currency shall be redeemed.

March 16, Mr. RANDALL called up the bill (No. 2450), and explained its nature. Mr. HEWETT spoke at length in favor of repealing the Resumption Act. He opposed the issue of silver as a subsidiary coin.

Mr. KELLEY followed in the same vein, showing the depreciation of silver from current reports, and predicting further depreciation. In the course of his remarks, he said: "The discussion is furnishing us with pregnant illustrations of the fact that money is a national institution; that it depends upon decrees of government, and that this is equally true whether it be of gold, of silver, or of paper, and that the special value of gold and silver is dependent on their use or disuse as money."

It was not until 1876 that the people and Congress began to understand that silver had been demonetized. The following remarks of a member from Indiana contained among the first announcements made in Congress on the subject.

Mr. LANDERS, of Indiana, opposed the bill. He said its object was to aid in carrying out the first section of the Resumption Act, against which every Democrat then in the House voted, and against which his constituents of both parties were opposed. The object of the Resumption Act was to change the character of the legal-tender currency into an interest-bearing debt. He was in favor of making United States notes and silver a legal-tender for all public dues.

June 21, 1876, the House joint resolution No. 109 being under consideration, Mr. LANDERS, of Indiana, said: "It is another effort in the interest of the bondholders against the people, and in the same direction as that of the act of 1869, and permit me to say almost as great a fraud upon the people as was that act. Why? Because, under acts by which the bonded debt of the Government was originally created, every dollar of its principal and interest could have justly been paid in silver, but because silver has now depreciated in value, it is insisted that we should not offer it in payment of that debt. That such is the case is no fault of ours. Our duty is to act fairly towards both the debtor and creditor class; and if, as some hold, the agreement was made to pay that debt, either in gold or silver, then, sir, it is at the option of the debtor to say in which kind of coin that payment shall be made. It will not injure the credit of the Government if we offer silver in payment of our debts. I do not understand that the credit either of individuals or of the Government is impaired by a strict compliance with contracts; and whatever they contracted to do they ought to fulfill and nothing more. * * * Mr. Speaker, I want members of this House distinctly to understand why it is that this effort is being made against silver. I hold that it is simply to increase the purchasing power of the bondholder, whose interest is paid him in gold."

June 28, 1876, Mr. LANDERS moved to amend an amendment of Mr. Randall to his bill by adding the following:

"*And it is further provided,* That the Secretary of the Treasury is directed to authorize the coinage of the standard silver dollar of the same weight and fineness in use January 1, 1861, and the said dollar shall be a legal-tender in payment of all debts, public and private."

Mr. RANDALL called for the previous question, and the yeas and nays were demanded. The yeas were 111, and the nays 55; not voting 123. So the amendment of Mr. Landers was adopted, and the bill as amended was agreed to—yeas 110, nays 45, not voting 134. The yeas were as follows:

Yeas—Messrs. Anderson, Ashe, Atkins, John H. Baker, Bland, Banks, Blount, Boone, Bradley, Bright, William R. Brown, Buckner, Horatio C. Burchard, Cabell, John H. Caldwell, William P. Caldwell, Campbell, Cannon, John B. Clarke, of Kentucky, John B. Clarke, jr., of Missouri, Conger, Cowan, Crouse, Culberson, Cutler, Davis, De Bolt, Denison, Dibrell, Douglas, Dunnell, Durham, Ellis, Evans, Faulkner, Felton, Forney, Franklin, Goodin, Gunter, Andrew H. Hamilton, Robert Hamilton, Henry R. Harris, John T. Harris, Hatcher, Haymond, Henderson, Hereford, Goldsmith W. Hewett, Holman, Hooper, House, Hunter, Hunton, Jenks, Thomas L. Jones, Kimball, Knott, Lamar, Franklin Landers, Leavenworth, Lewis, Lord, Luttrell, Lynde, L. A. Mackay, Magoon, Maish, McDill, McFarland, MacMahon, Metcalfe, Millikin, Mills, Neal, Odell, Randall, Rea, Reagan, James B. Reilly, Rice, Riddle, William M.

Robbins, Robinson, Sampson, Savage, Scales, Speakley, William E. Smith, Southard, Sparks, Spencer, Springer, Stevenson, Teese, Terry, Tufts, Waddell, Walsh, Erastus Wells, Whiting, Wigginton, Willard, Alpheus S. Williams, Jeremiah N. Williams, William B. Williams, James Wilson, Woodworth, Yeates and Young.

Nays—Messrs. Adams, Ainsworth, William H. Baker, Blackburn, Candler, Caswell, Davy, Eames, Foster, Frost, Frye, Hancock, Hardinburg, Benjamin W. Harris, Hendee, Hubbell, Frank Jones, Joyce, Lynch, Morgan, Norton, Oliver, Packer, Payne, William A. Phillips, Pierce, Piper, Platt, Potter, Rainey, John Robbins, Scleicher, Seelye, Smalls, A. Herr Smith, Strait, Tarbox, Thompson, Waldran, Alexander S. Wallace, John W. Wallace, Warren, White, Andrew Williams, and Wilshire.

Those not voting were 134 in number, but there is nothing to show how they would have voted if present.

The Senate disagreed to this and other amendments of the House, and a conference committee was appointed which agreed to throw out the amendment of Mr. Landers. The ground taken was, that the question of remonetization of silver had no necessary connection with that of issuing subsidiary coin for the immediate wants of the people.

July 14, when the report of the conference committee was under consideration in the Senate, Mr Bogy, of the committee, said he concurred in the report, although it fell short of what he desired to accomplish. He held that silver might properly be paid as interest on the public debt and for customs duties; but that he was willing to waive that right, and to make silver a legal-tender in all other cases, in other words, in payment of all private obligations.

Mr. Jones, of Nevada. I do not know why so promising a beginning should have so small an ending. I indulged the hope that the report of the committee would at least have been of such a character as to permit us to take the sense of the Senate on the transcendently important proposition of making money full weighted, full legal-tender money out of our great staple, silver; that we would have been permitted to record our votes for or against the restoration of the only legal unit of value in this country, namely, the silver dollar of the Constitution, of which we were deprived by an indirection in 1874. We were deprived of it in the interest of the creditors, and to the injury of the debtors of the country.

March 30, 1876.—In the Senate. The proposition of Mr. Sherman to demonetize the trade-dollar, which in the Revised Statutes had been classed with the subsidiary silver coin, and made a legal-tender to the amount of $5, being under consideration.

Mr. Sherman. There has been no silver dollar issued since 1853, *and my impression is that the law of 1853 did not confer the power to issue it.* The Senator thinks it did confer the power; but the law of 1873 cut off the power, in my judgment, if it existed. The dollar was practically dropped from our coinage system for the best possible reason; the same reason that the five-franc piece and the large coins of **England** have been dropped out of their currency, simply because it is inconvenient in size and form for ordinary coinage and ordinary business.

Mr. Jones, of Nevada. Allow me to suggest that the reason the dollar was dropped, and that no such silver coin has been coined since 1853, is because silver was at a premium at the then established ratio of gold, and nobody had any inducement to coin the silver dollar at that time.

The Senator from Nevada might have added that the act of 1853 did not confer the power to issue silver dollars, because that power was conferred by the act of 1792 and had never been taken away. The act of 1853 relates exclusively to the subsidiary coinage. Mr. Sherman, who introduced bills in 1868, 1870 and 1872, for the regulation of the mints and coinage, was very careful to insert a clause into each of them for the prohibition of the issue of silver dollars as legal-tender, and for the prohibition of the deposit of silver bullion in the mints for coinage. This precaution would have been supererogatory if the act of 1853 or any prior act had disallowed the coinage of silver dollars. The bill was recommitted to the Committee of Finance.

April 20, the Committee on Finance reported back the bill with a substitute providing for the coinage of the standard silver dollar of 412.8 grains, and making the same a legal-tender to the amount of twenty dollars.

Mr. Bogy, of Missouri, moved to make the silver dollar a legal-tender for all sums and receivable by the Government for duties on imports. He maintained that gold and silver were the constitutional currencies, and that there is no authority in the Federal Government to strip them of that character. He quoted Hamilton's report as Secretary of the Treasury, on the establishment of the mint, as follows:

" To annul the use of either of the metals as money is to abridge the quantity of the circulating medium of the world, and is liable to all the objections which arise from the comparison of the benefits of a full with the evils of a scanty circulation." Mr. Bogy also quoted Jefferson's indorsement of this statement of Hamilton, in the following words: " I return the report of the mint. I concur with you that the mint must stand upon both metals." Mr. Bogy quoted M. Wolowski, an eminent French writer, as follows: "To adopt one metal, gold, to the exclusion of the other, it is not merely as if they closed all existing mines of silver, but as if they suppressed in this regard the labor of all past ages. The sum total of the precious metals is reckoned at fifty milliards, [50,000,000,000 francs] one-half of gold and one-half of silver. If, by a stroke of the pen, they suppress one of these metals in the monetary service, they double the demand for the other metal to the ruin of all debtors."

April 24, Mr. Jones, of Nevada, made an able and elaborate speech in favor of silver.

April 25, the same subject being up for consideration, Mr. Bogy called attention to the fact that the act of February 12, 1873, did not demonetize silver, that it authorized the coinage of the subsidiary coins and the trade-dollar, and made them a legal-tender for sums not exceeding five dollars, and forbade the coinage of other silver coins. That the Revised Statutes by fraud demonetized silver The act authorizing the revision of the laws provided that none should be included but those in force December 1, 1873. Mr. Bogy then quotes the section, 3586, which has already been introduced into this historical sketch. He says of it : "This is a fraud. There was no law of that character existing at that day in this country.  *  *  * I think, furthermore, that section 3524 is equally a fraud, wherein it is stated that no foreign coin shall be a legal-tender in payment of debts."

Mr. Sherman concurred with Mr. Bogy as to the act of 1873, and said the dollar was a legal-tender unless it was demonetized by the Revised Statutes. But he, as well as Mr. Hooper and the Director of the Mint, had said that the silver dollars in consequence of their superior value to that of the gold dollar had all long ago disappeared, that they had been melted down or exported.

Mr. Logan insisted that the effect of the act of 1873 was to demonetize silver, since it forbade the coinage of the dollar, and there were no dollars in circulation. They had gone to the melting-pot. He asked Mr. Sherman how the demonetizing clause got into the Revised Statutes? Mr. Sherman said he did not know.

Mr. Howe inquired if the act of 1873 does "prohibit the coinage of the silver dollar other than the trade-dollar?"

Mr. Sherman admitted the fact. He said : "I have often been asked, not only in this Chamber, but outside, how comes it that the silver dollar was dropped from the coins of the country. *The answer is that in* 1873, *when these statutes were so carefully revised, the silver dollar as provided in the then existing law was worth more than a dollar in gold, more in the money markets of the world. There was no use then in issuing the dollar, because it would go into the melting-pot, being worth more than the gold dollar. That was the reason why the silver dollar was not provided for."*

Mr. Sherman failed to explain why it became necessary or proper to prohibit the coinage of the silver dollar when nobody wished it coined, when nobody would deposit silver bullion at the mint for coinage. This was the pretext. The true reason was that the foreign holders of American bonds called for it, and had sufficient influence on this side of the water to secure the desired result.

Mr. Sherman reiterated the above statement in reply to a question of Mr. Morton, and added that, by the law of 1837, the relation established between gold and silver was wrong ; that "we had undervalued silver by making one ounce of gold equal to sixteen ounces of silver, and, therefore, whenever silver was coined in the shape of dollars it went off, and so it was from 1853 to 1873."

The coinage of silver was prohibited in 1873, therefore, because no one would deposit his bullion for coinage ; and now the gold men wish to prohibit the coinage of silver because the owners of silver bullion and the people are anxious to have it coined.

Mr. LOGAN said : "Inasmuch as the country and the people have been deprived of the right to pay in silver coin by an act denying the right to coin the silver dollar, it being a legal-tender at the time for all amounts, the country will expect that when you restore that silver dollar you will let it be a legal-tender for all amounts just as it was up to 1873 ; and it is just and proper that it should. When you restore the silver dollar in this country and give it a place, and say its place shall only be for twenty, or ten, or five dollars, you deprive the people of this country of a right which they enjoyed from 1792 to 1873 ; and a right of which they have been deprived in a manner that they know not how. * * * So far as I am concerned—and I speak for myself alone—I will vote to strike out the twenty dollar limit and let the dollar stand as a legal-tender, as it did up to 1873, for all amounts."

June 8, 1876, Mr. MORRILL, of Vermont, spoke at length against silver as a legal-tender.

Mr. SHERMAN. "*For forty years, since 1834, the silver dollar, though in law a money of account, was in fact demonetized, because it was more valuable than the gold dollar. It was for that reason alone* the silver dollar was dropped from our coinage system. This is clearly stated in a report to the Senate of Mr. KNOX, Comptroller of the Currency, dated April 25, 1870. I read from his report as follows :

'The coinage of the silver dollar piece, the history of which is here given, is discontinued in the proposed bill. It is by law the dollar unit, and assuming the value of gold to be fifteen and one-half times that of silver, being about the mean ratio for the past six years, is worth in gold a premium of about three per cent. (its value being $1.0312), and intrinsically more than seven per cent. premium in our other silver coins ; its value thus being $1.0742. The present laws, consequently, authorize both a gold dollar unit and a silver dollar unit, differing from each other in intrinsic value. The present gold dollar piece is made the dollar unit in the proposed bill, and the silver dollar piece is discontinued. If, however, such a coin is authorized, it should be issued only as a *commercial dollar*, not as a standard unit of account, and of the exact value of the Mexican dollar, which is the favorite for circulation in China and Japan, and other Oriental countries.'

"This report," adds Mr. Sherman, "was the beginning of the voluminous documents which led to the revision of the mint laws of 1873. * * * The great revolution in the precious metals has occurred since, and now the practical question is, shall we avail ourselves of the extraordinary fall in silver to make the old silver dollar a full legal-tender, and thus to reduce the market value of our bonds, which we are not bound to pay, which are not due, and which we have not the ability to pay ; or shall we improve this opportunity offered us by an unforeseen event to redeem our depreciated notes without loss, and with the free and voluntary consent of the holder of them?''

It is a little singular that Mr. Sherman should insist on making the weight of the public debt heavier at a time when he states the country was unable to pay it. All that the most punctilious honor could demand was that the principal and interest of the bonds should be paid according to the terms of the contract, according to the letter of the law authorizing the issue of the bonds. There was no reason of state for "boosting" the public credit by a Quixotic and unprecedented magnanimity toward the public creditors. The bonds originally had been purchased with depreciated— greatly depreciated—United States notes. It was in the spirit of high honor and good faith that in 1869 they were made redeemable in coin—gold and silver coin—an obligation of honor which was merely inferential from circumstances, but which was not embraced in the bond. This was going far enough. But having secured this pledge, the bondholders, with unparalleled effrontery, demanded that none but gold coin—the standard coin of Great Britain, not that of America—should be paid them. They are now backed in this demand by the creditor class of this country. In the superserviceable zeal of the newly-fledged American champions of an exclusive gold standard, they seem to have closed their eyes to two facts, viz: First, that there are two parties to every contract involving an obligation to pay money, the debtor and the creditor; and that the rights of these parties before the law are equal. The creditor has a legal and equitable right to be paid at the time and place specified, and in the money or other thing named in the bond, the full amount of his debt, with interest. The debtor, also in law and equity, has the right to be shielded from any greater or different demand than that contained in the contract. In the case in hand it was as much the right of the debtor that gold should be demonetized when it became the dearer and scarcer metal as it was the right of the creditor that silver, the cheap metal, should be discarded as the legal-tender. But, in truth, there could be no justice in either demand. The contract called for the payment in coin, which consisted of gold and silver, and to vary the terms of the contract was to inflict gross injustice.

Another circumstance lost sight of, or ignored by the gold champions, was the fact that the demonetization of silver inflicted a grievous wrong upon the whole class of private debtors who had contracted debts when depreciated greenbacks constituted the sole money of the country. Resumption of specie payment in coin, in gold and silver, was, of itself, hard on this class who constitute at all times a majority of the people, but to go further and demand of them payment in gold, was high-handed extortion.

August 3, 1876, in the Senate, Mr. LOGAN introduced a bill (S.

No. 1026) for the issue of silver coin, and to make the silver dollar a legal-tender; which was read twice by its title, ordered to lie on the table and be printed.

April 2, 1876, in the House of Representatives, Mr. BLAND, of Missouri, in support of his bill for restoring silver as a legal-tender, said in reply to Mr. Casson, that "the bill that demonetized silver and perpetrated an injustice and fraud upon the people, was passed through this House without even being read, in spite of the call of the honorable gentleman at present serving as Speaker of the House [Mr. Kerr] for the reading of the bill. It was passed surreptitiously and without discussion, and was one of the grossest measures of injustice ever inflicted upon any people."

August 5th, the BLAND bill still pending, Mr. Hale, of Maine, intimated that a vote on the bill might be defeated by filibustering. Mr. Bland replied, denouncing the surreptitious manner in which silver was demonetized, and said he would insist on the previous question to the end of the session. Mr. PIERCE, of Boston, said the statement that the bill was surreptitiously carried through Congress was not true. It was nearly three years before Congress, and was printed thirteen times.

Mr. O'BRIEN, of Maryland, moved that the House adjourn.

Mr. TOWNSEND moved that the House adjourn till Thursday next, and demanded tellers. The yeas were 20, and the nays 116.

Mr. TOWNSEND called for the yeas and nays. The result was, yeas 4, nays 186.

The yeas and nays were then called on Mr. O'Brien's motion to adjourn. Yeas 2, nays 186.

But the morning hour had expired, and the bill went over.

August 8th, the same parties resorted to filibustering again, and prevented action on the bill until the expiration of the morning hour, and the bill thus fell through.

### FORTY-FOURTH CONGRESS, SECOND SESSION.

December 13, 1876, in the House of Representatives, Mr. Bland's bill (H. R. No 3635,) came up for consideration.

Mr. WILLARD said: "The gold sovereign of great Britain dominates only among 35,000,000 of people; the gold dollar or its equivalent is received by but 80,000,000, while the French franc (five franc) which corresponds nearly to the silver dollar, is in use and is the unit of value with 77,000,000; and the silver dollar in its various equivalents may be said to be used by more than 550,000,000 of the people of this globe."

Mr. Landers, of Indiana, said: "In 1834, the market value of gold and silver varied about 6 per cent., the silver being the lowest. The right of the debtor in those days was recognized. Albert Gallatin, and other distinguished statesmen, contended that it would be a great act of injustice to the debtor class to increase the value of silver, since the debt of the country was based upon that (it being cheaper), to make it correspond with the market value of gold. Their views were acknowledged to be correct, and Congress changed the gold eagle from 270 grains to 258, a reduction of 12 grains.''

Mr. GARFIELD opposed the bill. He quoted from Mr. Kelley's speech of January 9, 1872, in which the latter said: "It is imp,ssible to retain the double standard. The values of gold and silver continually fluctuate. You cannot determine this year what will be the relative values of gold and silver next year. They were 15 to 1 a short time ago. They are now 16 to 1. Hence all experience has shown that you must have one standard coin which shall be a legal-tender for all others.''

Mr. KELLEY admitted his change of opinion. He laid no claim to infallibility. He showed on high English authority that gold had risen in value as much as, or more than, silver had shrunk. He quoted the minutes of the Indian Board showing that prices in England and India, in silver, had not fallen. He now regarded the double standard as essential to the public welfare. He demanded the restoration of silver as a legal-tender, in the name of "the wronged and oppressed American people. They are in idleness and want by our legislation, shrinking the value of their labor and accumulated property. It is we who are dooming men of skill and industry to idleness and vagrancy. I ask that gentlemen to-day shall restore and enforce the law of 1869, which being an act to maintain the public credit, declared that all our obligations should be paid in coin of gold and silver. I ask you in the name of honor, of honesty, and justice to your constitutents, outraged and oppressed, to stand by the letter and spirit of the funding act of 1870, which in providing for the issue of four, four and a half and five per cent. bonds, provided that they should be paid in the then standard coin of the country. What was that standard coin? It was a gold dollar which was not the unit of value, and a silver dollar such as the substitute proposes, which was then, and had been from 1792, the unit of the monetary system of the United States.''

On the same day, December 13, 1876, a substitute for the original bill was adopted by yeas 167, nays 53, not voting 69. The substitute declares that from time to time there shall be coined at the mints silver dollars of the weight of 412½ grains of standard silver dollars as provided for in the act of January 18, 1837, and that the said dollar shall be a legal-tender for all debts, public and private, except where payment of gold coin is required by law. The substitute was numbered H. R. No. 4189.

The yeas were Messrs. Ainsworth, Anderson, Ashe, Atkins, Bagby, John H. Bagley, jr., John H. Baker, Banning, Bland, Blount, Boone, Bradford, Bradley, Bright, John Young Brown, William R. Brown, Buckner, H. C. Burchard, S. D. Burchard, Cabell, J. H. Caldwell, W. P. Caldwell, Campbell, Cannon, Carr, Cason, Caswell, Cate, Canfield, J. B. Clarke, of Ky., J. B. Clarke, jr., of Mo., Clymer, Collins, Conger, Cook, Cowan, Cox, Crounse, Culberson,

Cutler, Davis, Dibrell, **Durham**, Ellis, Evans, **Faulkner**, Felton, Finley, Forney, Fort, Foster, Franklin, **Fuller**, **Glover**, Goode, Gunter, A. H. Hamilton, Robert Hamilton, Hancock, **Hardenbergh, H. R. Harris**, J. T. Harris, Harrison, Hartridge, **Hartzell, Hatcher**, Haythorn, Haymond, Henderson, Hinkle, Hereford, **G. W. Hewett**, Holman, Hooker, Humphreys, Hunter, Hunton, Kelley, **Kimball**, Knott, **Lamar**, F. Landers, J. M. Landers, Lane, Leavenworth, Lewis, Luttrell, Lynde, Mackey, Magoon, McCrary, McDill, Mc-Farland, Milliken, Mills, Money, Monroe, Morgan, Mutchler, Neal, Odell, Oliver, Page, Payne, W. A. Phillips, Piper, Poppleton, Powell, Rea, Reagan, **J. Reilly**, Rice, **Riddle**, J. Robbins, W. M. Robbins, Roberts, Rusk, Sampson, Savage, **Scales, Speakley**, Singleton, Slemons, W. E. Smith, Southard, Sparks, **Spencer**, Springer, **Stanton**, Strait, Stenger, Stenson, Stone, Stowell, **Swan**, Teese, Terry, Thornburgh, Throckmorton, M. L. Townsend, **Tufts**, Turney, Van Vorhees, J. L. Vance, **R. B. Vance**, J. W. **Wallace**, Waddell, Waldron, G. C. Walker, A. S. Wallace, Walsh, **Watterson**, E. Wells, G. W. Wells, White, Whiting, Whitthorne, **Willard**, A. Williams, **C. G. Williams**, **J. N.** Williams, **W. B. Williams**, B. Wilson, J. Wilson, Woodworth, Yeates, and Young—167.

Nays—Messrs. Adams, G. A. Bagley, W. H. Baker, Ballou, **Bell**, Blair, Burleigh, Candler, Chittenden, Davy, Denison, Eames, **Ely**, Freeman, Frye, Garfield, Gibson, Hale, Haralson, B. W. Harris, **A. S. Hewett**, Hoar, Horkins, Hurd, **F. Jones**, Kasson, **Kehr, Levy**, Lynch, Maish, McDougall, Metcalfe, Miller, Nash, **Norton, O'Brien**, O'Neill, Packer, Pierce, Plaisted, Platt, Potter, **Schumaker, Seelye**, Sinnickson, A. H. Smith, Tarbox, Wait, **Warren, Alpheus S.** Williams, Willis, A. Wood, jr., and Fernando **Wood**.—53.

There were 69 absentees. There were no explanations given as to how they would have voted except in the case of Mr. House, of Tennessee, who would have voted " aye."

December 24, in the Senate. The above-described House bill was received in the Senate, and referred to the Committee on Finance.

January 16, 1877, the bill (H. R. No. 4189) was reported back from the Committee on Finance, by Mr. SHERMAN, without recommendation, and placed on the calendar, where it was allowed to sleep through the session.

### FORTY-FIFTH CONGRESS.

During the first session, commencing October 15, 1877, no less than twenty bills for the remonetization of the silver dollar were introduced in the House of Representatives by the following-named gentlemen: Messrs. Cox, of New York, Banning, Ewing, and Jones, of Ohio, Bright, of Tennessee, Hunter and Baker, of Indiana, Sparks, Harrison, Knapp, Fort, Townsend and Lathrop, of Illinois, Bland and Buckner, of Missouri, Phillips, of Kansas, Cummings and Oliver, of Iowa.

Mr. BLAND introduced two bills, the last being a substitute for the first. His substitute, introduced October 29, was referred to the

Committee on Banking and Currency. November 5th it was called up. On the motion to suspend the rules for the purpose of introducing and passing the bill, the yeas were 163, the nays 34; not voting, 93. It was passed without calling the yeas and nays. The substitute was H. R. No. 1013. It provided for coining the silver dollar of 412½ grains, for making it a legal-tender for all debts and dues, public and private, except where otherwise provided by contract. Any owner of silver bullion could deposit at the mints and have it coined. All inconsistent acts and parts of acts were repealed. It was sent to the Senate, and reported back November 21, with amendments.

December 6, 1877, Senator Stanley Matthews submitted resolutions reciting that the act of March 18, 1869, "entitled an act to strengthen the public credit," provided for the redemption of the Government bonds in coin of gold and silver; that, under the Refunding Act of July 14, 1870, the new bonds were made redeemable in gold and silver; and that the act of January 14, 1875, provided for the redemption of United States bonds in gold and silver coin; therefore,

" *Resolved*, That all the bonds of the United States are payable, principal and interest, in gold and silver," &c.

Mr. KERNAN, of New York, earnestly opposed the resolution.

[The statement in the resolution that the act of January 14, 1875, authorized the payment of United States bonds in silver coin is erroneous.]

Mr. BECK, of Kentucky, supported it.

Mr. DAWES, of Massachusetts, denied that the act of February 12, 1873, had been passed by improper means.

A motion was made by Mr. Allison, of Iowa, to lay aside the resolution, and take up the Bland silver bill. The motion was disagreed to.

December 10, 1877, Mr. Matthews presented the following resolution, which had been adopted in the winter of 1875–'76 by the legislature of Ohio:

" *Resolved*, By the general assembly of the State of Ohio, that common honesty to the tax-payers, the letter and spirit of the contract under which the great body of its indebtedness was assumed by the United States, and true financial wisdom, each and all, demand the restoration of the silver dollar to its rank as lawful money."

Mr. Matthews said the resolution was passed with great unanimity. There were but three negative votes in the House of Representatives and but one in the Senate.

The resolution of Mr. Matthews was adopted, yeas 43, nays 22; not voting 11. The preamble was passed, yeas 42, nays 20.

January 23, 1877, Mr. Blaine introduced a bill (Senate No. 597) to authorize the coinage of silver dollars and make them legal-tender. He afterwards explained that he was opposed to remonetizing the silver dollar of 4:2½ grains; but omitted on that occasion to state how many grains he would add.

February 7, 1878, Mr. Blaine proposed to make the silver dollar consist of 425 grains of standard silver, with unlimited coinage, and a legal-tender for all sums.

February 13, 1878, in the Senate, Mr. HEREFORD, of West Virginia, recited the circumstances of the passage of the Demonetization Act in February, 1873, through the House of Representatives ; that it was forced through, viz: the substitute of Mr. Hooper, without having been read or printed. He quoted from a speech made by Mr. Garfield, in the fall of 1877, in a popular assembly, in which that gentleman said he was ashamed to confess that he did not know what was in the bill demonetizing silver when it passed—that it was put through upon the faith of the chairman, Mr. Hooper.

Mr. VOORHEES said : "Never since the foundation of this Government has a law of such vital and tremendous import, or indeed, of any importance at all, crawled into our statute books so furtively and so noiselessly as this. Its enactment was as completely unknown to the people, and indeed, to four-fifths of Congress itself, as the presence of a burglar in a house at midnight is to its sleeping inmates."

In referring to the act of March, 1869, Mr. MORTON, the able Senator from Indiana, said : "We should do foul injustice to the Government and the people of the United States, after we have sold these bonds at an average for not more than sixty cents on the dollar, now to make a new contract for the benefit of the holders."

February 15, 1878, Mr. INGALLS, of Kansas, said :

If we are to have a monometallic standard, I believe silver to be immeasurably preferable to gold. It is less subject to fluctuation ; its production is more steady ; its cost more uniform. * * Gold is the money of monarchs. * * If we contracted to pay in gold we must do so, though it leave us beggars. But did we so agree ? The act of February 25, 1862, authorizing the issue of five-twenty bonds provides that the interest shall be paid not in gold, but in coin. The act also provides that duties on imports shall be paid not in gold, but in coin. The same act created the sinking fund, payable not in gold, but in coin. The act of February 17, 1862, makes its obligations payable not in gold, but in coin. The act of March 3, 1863, providing for the issue of $900,000,000 makes them payable not in gold, but in coin. The act of March 3, 1864, for a loan of $200,000,-000 makes it payable not in gold, but in coin. The act of June 30, 1864, to borrow $400,000,000 makes it payable not in gold, but coin. The act of March 3, 1865, for $600,000,000, makes them payable in "coin or other lawful money," not gold but coin or greenbacks. The act of March 18, 1869, "An act to strengthen the public credit," &c., solemnly pledges "the faith of the United States" to the payment in coin or its equivalent of all obligations, unless it is where an express stipulation is to the contrary."

The Senator might have added that the funding act of 1870 provides for the redemption of the bonds, not in gold, but in coin. He proceeds to remark : " The odious cant about repudiation is a knavish device to intimidate a people who have always respected their obligations." The great journals of Europe entertain no such opinions. The London *Times* recently said: " It could in no sense be called repudiation if silver were made the sole standard of the United States to-morrow."

Mr. LAMAR said he had the painful duty to perform of presenting the resolutions of the State of Mississippi, which he asked to be read. They instructed the Senators and requested the Representatives to vote for the remonetization of silver.

On the same day, February 15, 1878, the following interesting colloquy took place in regard to the passage of the act of February 12, 1873, which prohibited the coinage of the silver dollar :

Mr. VOORHEES. Was the gentleman from Maine equally ignorant with the rest of us? If he will say he was we shall be somewhat content.

Mr. BLAINE. I do not mean ignorance of this particular provision, but I mean ignorance of its effect. He had just admitted, while defending the good faith of those who were active in support of the the bill, that the truth is, nobody cared about it ; there was no great attention called to it. We are all a great deal wiser about it to-day than we were then. I remember a little incident when Dr. Johnson, I believe, in the first edition of his dictionary, defined the pastern joint of a horse to be the knee, and a lady asked him why he did that. Said the gruff old moralist : " Ignorance, madam ; pure ignorance." Now let us be equally frank. We were in pure and absolute ignorance of the whole subject. It was not known."

[This confession of ignorance does credit to Mr. Blaine's candor but it has no application to the active movers of the measure nor to the revisers and their backers who fraudulently interpolated the section into the Revised Statutes which demonetized silver.]

In reply to Mr. Voorhees, Mr. BLAINE continued : " I think now, very clearly, with the light before me, that it was a great blunder. * * I did not know anything that was in the bill at all. As I have before said, little was known or cared on the subject." [Laughter.]

Mr. BLAINE (who was Speaker when the bill passed the House) in turn, asked Mr. Voorhees, who was on the floor of the House, as a member, at the time, if he knew the nature of the bill?

Mr. VOORHEES. I very frankly say that I did not.

Mr. THURMAN. While stating that the act of February 12, 1873, did not demonetize silver, but stopped the coinage of the silver dollar, said : " I cannot say what took place in the House, but I know, when the bill was pending in the Senate, we thought it was simply a bill to reform the mint, regulate coinage, and fix up one thing and another, and there is not a single man in the Senate, I think, unless a member of the committee from which the bill came, who had the slightest idea that it was even a squint toward demonetization."

No Senator rose to controvert this statement of Mr. Thurman. His former colleague, Mr. Sherman, who had introduced the bill and steered it through the Senate, if present, might have told all about it, but he was now a member of Mr. Hayes' cabinet.

Mr. Kelley, of Pennsylvania, March 9, 1878, said that "though the chairman of the Committee on Coinage, I was as ignorant of the fact that it would demonetize the silver dollar, or of its dropping the silver dollar from our system of coins, as were those distinguished Senators, Messrs. Blaine and Voorhees," &c. [But here Mr. Kelley's memory was at fault, for he had advocated that very feature of the demonetization bill.] Messrs. Cannon and Burchard, of Illinois, avowed their ignorance of what the bill contained. Mr. Allison, of Iowa, said the original bill had been "doctored;" but disclaimed using the word in "an offensive sense." In other words, he used offensive words in a Pickwickian sense. Senator Howe compared the act to the guilt of robbing the people of two hundred millions.

The same day, February 15, 1878, the bill (Bland bill for the re-monetization of silver) was adopted in the Senate by yeas, 48, nays 21, absent 7.

The yeas were Messrs. Allison and Kirkwood, of Iowa, Armstrong and Cockrell, of Missouri, Bailey, of Tennessee, Beck and McCreery, of Kentucky, Booth, of California, Bruce, of Mississippi, Cameron and Howe, of Wisconsin, Cameron and Wallace, of Pennsylvania, Chaffee and Teller, of Colorado, Coke and Maxey, of Texas, Conover and Jones, of Florida, Davis and Oglesby, of Illinois, Davis and Hereford, of West Virginia, Dennis, of Maryland, Dorsey and Garland, of Arkansas, Eustis and Kellogg, of Louisiana, Gordon, of Georgia, Grover, of Oregon, Ingalls and Plumb, of Kansas, Johnston and Withers, of Virginia, Jones, of Nevada, Ferry, of Michigan, Matthews and Thurman, of Ohio, McDonald and Voorhees, of Indiana, McMillan and Windom, of Minnesota, Merriman, of North Carolina, Morgan and Spencer, of Alabama, Paddock and Saunders, of Nebraska, Salisbury of Delaware.—48.

The nays were Messrs. Anthony and Burnside, of Rhode Island, Barnum, of Connecticut, Bayard, of Delaware, Blaine and Hamlin, of Maine, Christiancy, of Michigan, Conkling and Kernan, of New York, Dawes and Hoar, of Massachusetts, Edmunds and Morrill, of Vermont, Lamar, of Mississippi, McPherson and Randolph, of New Jersey, Mitchell, of Oregon, Rollins and Wadleigh, of New Hampshire, Sargent, of California, Whyte, of Maryland.—21.

Absent—Messrs. Butler and Patterson, of South Carolina, Eaton, of Connecticut, Harris, of Tennessee, Hill, of Georgia, Ransom, of North Carolina, Sharon, of Nevada.—7.

Of these, it was stated on the floor, by colleagues, or by themselves, that Messrs. Harris, Patterson and Ransom, if present or unpaired, would have voted yea; and that Messrs. Butler, Eaton and Hill would have voted nay. Mr. Sharon had no pair but, if present, would have voted yea, so that a full vote would have been yeas 52, nays 24.

The bill went back to the House with the Senate amendments, and on the 21st of February, after a long debate, Mr. Hewitt, of New York, moved to lay the bill and amendments on the table. The yeas and nays were called for by Mr. Sayler, of Ohio. The yeas were 71, and the nays 205, not voting 16.

Upon the adoption of the amendment which limited the amount of silver to be coined monthly to a minimum of two million dollars and a maximum of four millions, the bullion to be purchased by the head of the mint, the yeas were 203, the nays 72, not voting 17. Many friends of the original bill voted against this amendment, and most of its opponents for it.

Upon the adoption of the amendment providing for the silver commission, the yeas were 196, the nays 71, and the absentees 25. The vote, yea and nay, on this amendment, came from the same parties which cast the vote on the limitation of silver coinage. The amendments of the Senate were all concurred in, and the bill was signed February 25, 1878.

Upon Mr. Hewitt's motion to lay the bill on the table, which was the only test vote upon the unlimited coinage of silver at the wish of depositors of silver, the yeas and nays were as follows:

Yeas—Messrs. Bacon, Bagley, William H. Baker, Ballou, Banks, Bisbee, Blair, Bliss, Briggs, Camp, Campbell, Chittenden, Claflin, Alvan A. Clark, Covert, Crapo, Horace Davis, Denison, Dwight, Eames, Eickhoff, I. Newton Evans, Field, Freeman, Frye, Garfield, Gibson, Hale, Hardenburg, Harmer, Benj. W. Harris, Hart, Abram S. Hewitt, Hungerford, James, Frank Jones, Jorgensen, Joyce, Ketcham, Lapham, Leonard, Lindsay, Lockwood, Loring, McCook, Morse, Muller, O'Neil, Peddie, Potter, Pugh, Quin, Reed, William W. Rice, George D. Robinson, Ross, Schleicher, Sinnicksen, Starin, Stenger, Stewart, Swan, Veeder, Wait, Ward, Warner, Watson, A. S. Williams, Andrew Williams, James Williams, Wood.—71.

Nays—Messrs. Ackler, Aiken, Aldrich, Atkins, John H. Baker, Banning, Bayne, Beebe, Bell, Benedict, Bicknell, Blackburn, Bland, Blount, Boone, Bouck, Boyd, Bragg, Brantano, Brewer, Bridges, Bright, Brogden, Browne, Buckner, Bundy, Burchard, Burdick, Butler, Cabell, Cain, John W. Caldwell, W. P. Caldwell, Calkins, Chandler, Cannon, Carlisle, Caswell, Chalmers, Clark, of Missouri, Rush Clark, Clark, of Kentucky, Clymer, Cobb, Cole, Collins, Conger, Cook, Jacob D. Cox, Samuel S. Cox, Cravens, Crittenden, Culberson, Cummings, Cutler, Danford, Davidson, Joseph J. Davis, Deering, Dibrell, Dickey, Douglas, Dunnell, Eden, Elam, Ellis, Ellsworth, Errett, James L. Evans, John H. Evins, Ewing, Finley, Forney, Fort, Foster, Franklin, Fuller, Garth, Ganse, Giddings, Glover, Goode, Gunter, Hamilton, Hanna, Henry R. Harris, John T. Harris, Harrison, Hartridge, Hartzell, Haskell, Hatcher, Hayes, Hazleton, Henderson, Henkle, Henry, Herbert, G. W. Hewett, Hiscock, Hooker, House, Hubbell, Humphrey, Hunter, Hunton, Ittner, James J. Jones, John S. Jones, Keifer, Kelley, Kenna, Killinger,

Kimmel, Knapp, Knott, Landers, Lathrop, Ligon, Luttrell, **Lynde,**
Mackey, Manning, Marsh, Martin, McGowan, McKenzie, **McKinley,**
McMahon, Metcalfe, Mills, Mitchell, Money, Monroe, Morgan, **Morri**-
son, Muldrow, Neal, Oliver, Overton, Page, G. W. Patterson, **T. M.**-
Patterson, Phelps, Phillips, Pollard, Pound, Price, Pridemore,
Rainey, Randolph, Rea, Reagan, Reilly, Riddle, Robbins, Roberts,
Robertson, Milton S. Robinson, Ryan, Sampson, Sapp, Sayler, Scales,
Sexton, Shallenberger, Shelley, Singleton, Slemons, Smalls, Southard,
Sparks, Springer, Steele, Stephens, John W. Stone, Joseph C. Stone,
Strait, Thompson, Thornburgh, Throckmorton, Amos Townsend, R.
W. Townshend, Tucker, Turner, Turney, Vance, Van Vorhees, Wad-
dell, **Walker,** Walch, Welch, Harry White, Michael **D.** White,
Whitthorne, Wigginton, C. G. **Williams,** Jerry N. Williams, Rich-
ard Williams, Albert S. Willis, Willitts, Wilson, Wren, Wright,
Yates.—205.

There were only 16 absentees.

### COURSE OF MR. SHERMAN.

In the course of the debate, January 15, 1878, Mr. Voorhees quoted
a resolution adopted by the Republican convention of Ohio in 1868,
in which the convention expressed its deliberate "conviction that
according to the laws under which the 5-20 bonds were issued, said
bonds should be paid in the currency of the country which may be
legal-tenders when the Government shall be prepared to redeem such
bonds." "And on this doctrine," said Mr. Voorhees, "the present Chief Magistrate, and his secretary, took their stand only nine
years ago. Not only so, but Secretary Sherman, who now in his recent report warns us against repudiation, then gave in a letter, dated
March 30, 1868, and widely published, his idea of what constituted a
repudiator." Mr. Sherman's letter is as follows:

"UNITED STATES SENATE CHAMBER,
"WASHINGTON, *March* 30, 1868.

"DEAR SIR: I was glad to receive your letter. My personal inter-
ests are the same as yours, but, like you, I do not intend to be influ-
enced by them. My construction of the law is the result of careful
examination, and I feel quite sure an impartial court would confirm
it if the case should be tried before a court. I send you my views as
fully stated in a speech. Your idea that we propose to repudiate or
violate a promise, when we offer to redeem the "principal" in legal-
tenders, is erroneous. I think the bondholder violates his promise
when he refuses to take the same kind of money he paid for the
bonds. If the case is to be tested by the law I am right, if it is to
be tested by Jay Cooke's advertisements, I am wrong. I hate repudiation, or anything like it, but we ought not to be deterred from
what is right for fear of undeserved epithets. If under the law as
it stands the holders of five-twenties can only be paid in gold, the
bondholder can demand only the kind of money he paid, then he is
a repudiator and extortioner to demand money more valuable than
he gave. Yours truly,                     "JOHN SHERMAN."

On the 30th of January, 1878, Mr. Christiancy, of Michigan, undertook the defense of Mr. Sherman's consistency, and read a letter from that gentleman, written ten years later than the above, which attempts to reconcile the statements in the above letter with his position as the leader in the movement to redeem the public debt in an exclusively gold currency. In his later letter, addressed to Senator Morrill, of Vermont, and dated January 26, 1878, Mr. Sherman says:

"I have noticed that my casual letter to Dr. Mann, of the date of March 30, 1868, inclosing a speech made by me, has frequently been used to prove that I have changed my opinion since that time as to the right of the United States to pay the principal of the 5-20 bonds in legal-tenders. This would not be very important, if true, but it is not true, as I never have changed my opinion as to the technical legal right to redeem the principal of the 5-20 bonds in legal-tenders, but, as you know and correctly state, have always insisted that we could not avail ourselves of this legal right until we complied in all respects with the legal and moral obligations imposed by the legal-tender note, to redeem it in coin on demand, or to restore the right to convert it into an interest-bearing Government bond. The grounds of this opinion are very fully stated in the speech made February 27, 1868, referred to in the letter to Dr. Mann, and in a report on the Funding Bill made by me from the Committee on Finance, December 17, 1867. If my letter is taken in connection with the speech, which it inclosed, and to which it expressly referred, it will be perceived that my position then is entirely consistent with what it is now; and time has proven that if the report of the Committee on Finance had been adopted we would long since have reached the coin standard with an enormous saving of interest and without impairing the public credit.

"My position was that, while the legal-tender act made United States notes a legal-tender for all debts, public and private, except for customs duties and interest of the public debt, yet we could not honestly compel the public creditors to receive United States notes in payment of bonds until we made good the pledge of the public faith to pay the notes in coin. The promise was printed on the face of the notes when issued, was repeated in several acts of Congress, and was declared valid and obligatory by the Supreme Court."

The sin of inconsistency consists, not in the change of opinion, but in the denial of it, and the attempt to explain it away. Indeed, a frank confession of change generally has the effect of inspiring respect and, confidence, and, as in the case of Mr. Kelley, of gaining credit for increasing wisdom.

Mr. Sherman made a great mistake in referring his correspondents to his old speeches, for they are they which condemn him. In his speech of February 27, 1868, he stated that the funded debt was $1,613,442,650, of which all except about $200,000,000 was in five-twenties six per cent. bonds, and that the seven-thirties would be refunded before the first of July. There was, also, he said, a floating debt, consisting chiefly of compound interest notes, amounting to $106,042,949. He urged the importance of refunding the whole debt, at a lower rate of interest, before the resumption of specie payments should take place, and quoted a speech of his delivered April 22, 1866, in which he said :

" Every one desires to resume specie payments. Before we return to specie payments this debt ought to be funded. It cannot be funded on as favorable terms after we return to specie payments. The very abundance of the currency obviously enable us to fund the debt at a low rate of interest ; *and it is just and right as this debt was contracted upon an inflated currency, that upon that same currency the debt ought to be funded in its permanent form.*"

The obvious meaning of this is, that the six per cent. five-twenties should be paid off in greenbacks before greenbacks were at par with gold and silver—before the Government was able and ready to redeem them in coin. On the theory of Mr. Sherman, the bondholders were bound to take them, and of course the debt could have been refunded more cheaply with uncurrent greenbacks than with coin.

But, again, Mr. Sherman said in speech of February 27, 1868, that the funding process should have begun two years before, when the paper currency was still more abundant ; and he deprecated the policy of contraction that had been pursued by Mr. McCulloch. But " that policy was entered into, and by the act of April 12, 1866, *passed against my earnest protest*, we gave to the Secretary of the Treasury almost unlimited power over the currency and over the public debt. * * * Within two years he contracted the legal-tender currency $160,000,000, and the plain United States notes over forty million. He also converted all the floating currency debt into gold interest bonds. At the time this law was passed, April 12, 1866, the total amount of five-twenty bonds was $666,000,000 ; and the great mass of the debt was in what are called currency obligations, the principal of which, undoubtedly, could have been paid in currency."

In the revised speech, under the heading, " How five-twenties are redeemable," Mr. Sherman took issue with Mr. Edmunds, the latter holding that the bonds were redeemable in gold. Mr. Sherman quoted the language of the act of February 25, 1862, which authorized the issue of $150,000,000 of United States notes, and $500,000,000 of bonds. The act declares that " such notes herein authorized shall be received in payment of all taxes, internal duties, excises, debts, and demands of every kind due to the United States, except duties on imports, and of all claims and demands against the United States of every kind whatsoever, except for interest upon bonds and notes, which shall be paid in coin ; and shall also be lawful money, and a legal-tender in payment of all debts, public and private, within the United States, except duties on imports and interest as aforesaid." Mr. Sherman asks triumphantly : " Does not this act, in so many words, declare that, while coin shall be paid for the interest of the public debt, yet the notes provided by this act shall be a lawful tender in payment of all public debts?''

Mr. Sherman said he approved the course pursued by Secretary Chase, in redeeming bonds issued prior to the act of February 25, 1862, in coin, on the ground that coin was at that day the only lawful currency. The pending act, he maintained, was not a threat. " It is only an offer of new bonds at lower interest for the old. If not accepted, then the next Congress, or the present Congress at its next session, will decide the question, *whether the redemption of these bonds shall be postponed to some indefinite future, when we may be able to pay gold for what we received in depreciated paper.*" It will be noticed that in the closing sentence of Mr. Sherman's letter to Dr. Mann of 1868 he declared that the bondholder is a " repudiator and an extortioner to demand money more valuable than he gave."

## OTHER IMPORTANT FACTS.

The following summary of important facts, bearing upon the silver question, are appended to the foregoing historical sketch for the convenience of the reader:

### IN THE CONGRESS OF THE CONFEDERATION

February 21, 1782. The Congress adopted an ordnance for the establishment of a mint.

July 6, 1785; it was "*Resolved*, That the money unit of the United States of America be one dollar." On the question of its adoption every member voted aye.

" That the smallest coin be of copper, of which two hundred shall pass for one dollar.

" That the several pieces shall increase in a decimal ratio."

August 8, 1786, on the report of the Board of Treasury—

" *Resolved*, That the standard of the United States of America for gold and silver shall be eleven parts fine and one part alloy.

" That the money unit of the United States, being by the resolve of Congress of the 6th July, 1785, a dollar shall contain of fine silver 375.64 grains.

" That the money of account, to correspond with the division of coins, agreeably to the above resolve, proceed in a decimal ratio.

" That betwixt the dollar and the lowest copper coin, as fixed by the resolve of Congress of the 6th July, 1785, there shall be three silver coins and one copper coin."

These silver coins were to be a half dollar of 187.82 grains of pure metal, a double dime of 75.128 grains of fine silver, and a dime of 37.564 grains of fine silver. The copper coins were to be a cent and half cent. Two pounds and a quarter, avoirdupois weight, of copper constituted one hundred cents.

Two gold coins were provided for. One containing 246.268 grains of fine gold, equal to ten dollars, to be stamped with the impression

of the American eagle, and to be called an eagle, and one containing
123.134 grains of fine gold, equal to five dollars, and to be called a
half eagle.

"That the mint price of a pound troy weight of uncoined silver,
eleven parts fine and one part alloy, shall be nine dollars, nine
dimes, and two cents.

"That the mint price of a pound troy weight of uncoined gold
eleven parts fine and one part alloy, shall be two hundred and nine
dollars, seven dimes, and seven cents." .

The mint price of silver, as above stated, although copied from the
journals of the Congress, is a palpable error, either of the author,
the engrosser of the ordnance, or the printer. I believe it was
afterwards corrected, but I now fail to find the correction.

The same ordnance provided that "the Board of Treasury report
a draft of an ordnance for the establishment of a mint."

Nothing seems to have been done under the similar ordnance of
1782 ; and no coinage took place while the articles of confederation
were in force.

## UNDER THE CONSTITUTION.

ARTICLE I, SEC. 10. No State shall coin money ; emit bills of credit;
make anything but gold and silver a tender in payment of debts.

## THE ACT OF APRIL 2, 1792.

SECTION 9 provides for gold, silver, and copper coins. The gold
eagles to contain 247$\frac{4}{8}$ grains of pure gold, or 270 grains of standard gold. Half and quarter eagles to contain like proportions. Dollars or units each to be of the value of a Spanish milled dollar, " as
the same is now current," to contain 371$\frac{1}{4}$ grains of pure, or 416
grains of standard silver. Half dollars, quarters, dimes, and half
dimes to contain like proportions of the metal. The cent to contain
eleven pennyweights of copper.

SEC. 11. The proportion of silver to gold in value, 15 to 1 in quantity or weight. The standard gold to consist of eleven parts pure
metal to one part alloy. The alloy to consist of silver and copper—
not above half silver.

SEC. 13. The standard for silver 1485 parts fine to 179 parts alloy,
the alloy to consist of copper.

SECTION 14 made it lawful for any person or persons to deposit gold
or silver bullion at the mint, for coinage, free of charge.

## THE ACT OF JUNE 18, 1834.

SECTION 1. Each eagle to contain 232 grains of pure gold, and 258
grains of standard gold. Half and quarter eagles to contain like
proportions of pure and mixed metals, and these coins, when of full
weight, to be received in payment of all debts. If under weight then
to be received according to weight.

## The Act of January 18, 1837.

Sec. 8. That the standard for both gold and silver coins of the United States shall hereafter be such that of one thousand parts by weight, nine hundred shall be of pure metal and one hundred of alloy ; and the alloy of silver coins shall be of copper, and the alloy of the gold coins shall be of copper and silver, provided that the silver do not exceed one-half of the whole alloy.

Sec. 9. That of the silver coins, the dollar shall be of the weight of four hundred and twelve and one-half grains. The half dollar, the quarter, the dime, and half dime were to be made of like proportions of the metals. These silver coins it was disclared, "shall be legal-tenders of payment, according to their nominal value, for any sums whatever."

Sec. 10. *Provided*, That the weight of the gold coins should be the same as they were fixed in the act of 1834.

Sec. 12. The weight of the copper cent to be 168 grains, and that of the half cent, 84 grains.

Sec. 14. Gold and silver bullion deposited at the mint to be coined for the benefit of the depositor.

Sec. 18. Certain charges fixed for assaying bullion below stand-ard, for toughening, when necessary, and for the copper and silver used as alloy. These charges not to exceed the actual expenses.

### Act of March 3, 1849.

Section 1 declares that, from time to time, there shall be struck and coined double eagles, each of the value of twenty dollars or units, and gold dollars, each to be of the value of one dollar or unit.

Sec. 2. These gold coins to be a legal-tender.

### The Act of March 3, 1851, to Modify the Rates of Postage.

Section 11 provides for the coinage of a three cent piece, composed of three parts silver and one part copper.

### Act of February 21, 1853.

Section 1 reduces the weight of the half dollar to 192 grains ; and the quarter, dime, and half dime, to be, respectively, one-half, one-fifth, and one-tenth of the half dollar.

Section 2 declares that the silver coins issued in conformity with the above section shall be legal-tender for sums not exceeding five dollars.

Sec. 3. The treasurer of the mint authorized to purchase bullion for the coinage of these coins.

Sec. 4. The amount coined into these subsidiary coins to be regu-lated by the Secretary of the Treasury.

Sec. 5. No private deposits of bullion for coinage into these halves, quarters, etc., to be permitted.

Section 7 provides for the coinage of gold three dollar pieces, of the standard weight and fineness.

## ACT OF FEBRUARY 25, 1862.

SECTION 1 authorizes the Secretary of the Treasury to issue $150,-000,000 of United States notes.

SECTION 2 authorized the Secretary to fund the notes and floating debt of the United States, and to that end the Secretary was authorized to issue, on the credit of the United States, coupon or registered bonds to an amount not exceeding five hundred millions of dollars, redeemable at the pleasure of the United States after five years, and payable twenty years from date, and bearing interest at the rate of six per cent. per annum, payable semi-annually in coin.

The notes were made " receivable in payment of all taxes, internal duties, excises, debts, and demands of every kind due to the United States, except duties on imports, and of all claims and demands against the United States, of every kind whatsoever, except for interest upon bonds and notes, which shall be paid in coin, and shall also be lawful money and a legal-tender in payment of all debts, public and private, within the United States, except duties on imports and interest as aforesaid.

SECTION 5 enacts that the duties on imported goods shall be paid in coin ; and that the coin shall be applied to the payment—First, of the interest of the bonds and notes of the United States ; and

Second, To the purchase or payment of 1 per centum of the entire debt of the United States, to be made in each fiscal year after the 1st day of July, 1862, which is to be set apart as a sinking fund, and the interest of which shall, in like manner, be applied to the purchase or payment of the public debt as the Secretary of the Treasury shall, from time to time, direct.

The subsequent acts affecting the silver question have been given, in substance, in the course of the historical sketch, and need not be repeated.

---

*Facts in regard to gold and silver in the world, taken from a recent annual report of the Director of the Mint.*

Total circulation of gold and silver coin in the world :

| | |
|---|---:|
| Gold | $3,293,606,836 |
| Silver | 2,754,611.080 |
| Total specie in circulation | 6,048,217.916 |
| Add total in banks and Government treasuries | 1,959,571,764 |
| Total gold and silver coin | 8,007,789,680 |

*Estimate of the aggregate production of the precious metals in all countries from A. D. 1493 to 1875.—American Almanac copying a German authority.*

| | |
|---|---:|
| Silver | $6,159,241,948 |
| Gold | 4,643,087,395 |
| Total | 10,802,329,343 |

This estimate includes all the gold and silver that has been dug out of the earth since the year 1493, or until 1875. The metals are gradually consumed like other commodities, by the various uses to which they are applied; and it is probable that an amount has in this way been lost quite equal to that on hand in all countries when America was discovered.

If this estimate of the wear and tear of the precious metals be correct, the amount that has been mined during the past four centuries is about equal to the amount now extant; and that of the $10,802,-329,343 in value, there would be $2,799,539,663 in value in use in the arts. The greatest part of the value of the precious metals is, therefore, due to the use that is made of them as money.

Secretary Manning, in his official report, bore testimony to the value of silver in the statement that "the statisticians all agree that silver is 54 per cent. of the monetary metals of mankind," and that "gold is fairly computed to be about 46 per cent. of the two monetary metals of mankind." That "gold from the mines of all the world has doubled in quantity within thirty-five years; silver about doubling in the last hundred years." "In the United States," says the Secretary, "the gold product during the last forty years has been 72 per cent. of the total amount of precious metals mined, and the silver 28 per cent., and it is only during the last fiscal year that the silver product has exceeded that of gold." These facts would show that silver is the more stable in value of the two metals, so far as the value is affected by the amount produced.

## The Late Act.

The recent act of Congress, entitled "An act directing the purchase of silver bullion and the issue of Treasury notes thereon, and for other purposes," treats silver as a commodity on which the public Treasury gives its notes to the depositors. The process of coinage is to go on as heretofore to the end of the present fiscal year, after which it is to cease, except in the contingency of the notes being presented for redemption. The provision that four and a half million ounces of silver shall be bought monthly by the Government, and that United States notes be issued in payment for it, will greatly increase the market price of silver, and thus demonstrate that the fall in price has been due to demonetization, but the arrangement is far from satisfying the people, who demand free coinage on a perfect equality with gold. And they will have it yet. The following are the essential portions of the act:

An act directing the purchase of silver bullion and the issue of Treasury notes thereon, and for other purposes.

"*Be it enacted by the Senate and House of Representatives of the United States of America in Congress assembled,* That the Secretary of the Treasury is hereby directed to purchase, from time to time, silver bullion to the aggregate amount of four million five hundred thousand ounces, or so much thereof as may be offered in each month, at the market price thereof, not exceeding one dollar for three hundred and seventy-one and twenty-five hundredths grains of pure silver, and to issue in payment for such purchases of silver bullion Treasury notes of the United States to be prepared by the Secretary of the Treasury, in such form and of such denominations, not less than one dollar nor more than one thousand dollars, as he may prescribe, and a sum sufficient to carry into effect the provisions of this act is hereby appropriated out of any money in the Treasury not otherwise appropriated.

"Sec. 2. That the Treasury notes issued in accordance with the provisions of this act shall be redeemable on demand, in coin, at the Treasury of the United States, or at the office of any assistant treasurer of the United States, and when so redeemed may be reissued; but no greater or less amount of such notes shall be outstanding at any time than the cost of the silver bullion and the standard silver dollars coined therefrom, then held in the Treasury purchased by such notes; and such Treasury notes shall be a legal-tender in payment of all debts, public and private, except where otherwise expressly stipulated in the contract, and shall be receivable for customs, taxes, and all public dues, and when so received may be reissued; and such notes, when held by any national banking association, may be counted as a part of its lawful reserve. That upon demand of the holder of any of the Treasury notes herein provided for the Secretary of the Treasury shall, under such regulations as he may prescribe, redeem such notes in gold or silver coin, at his discretion, it being the established policy of the United States to maintain the two metals on a parity with each other upon the present legal ratio, or such ratio as may be provided by law.

" Sec. 3. That the Secretary of the Treasury shall each month coin two million ounces of the silver bullion purchased under the provisions of this act into standard silver dollars until the first day of July, eighteen hundred and ninety-one, and after that time he shall coin of the silver bullion purchased under the provisions of this act as much as may be necessary to provide for the redemption of the Treasury note herein provided for, and any gain or seigniorage arising from such coinage shall be accounted for and paid into the Treasury.

" Sec. 4. That the silver bullion purchased under the provisions of this act shall be subject to the requirements of existing law and the regulations of the mint service governing the methods of determining the amount of pure silver contained, and the amount of charges or deductions, if any, to be made."

* 9 7 8 3 7 4 3 3 2 0 4 7 5 *